heartbeat!

Living with Passion in the Word of Christ

heartbeat!

Living with Passion in the Word of Christ

BY STEPHEN J. CARTER

CONCORDIA PUBLISHING HOUSE · SAINT LOUIS

Dedication

This book is dedicated to our seven grandchildren: Brendan, Hailey, Jonah, Josiah, Jesse, Jeremiah and James so that God's heartbeat will help them live with passion in the Word of Christ!

Published by Concordia Publishing House
3558 S. Jefferson Avenue, St. Louis, MO 63118-3968
1-800-325-3040 · www.cph.org

Manufactured in the United States of America

1 2 3 4 5 6 7 8 9 10   20 19 18 17 16 15 14 13 12 11

Prologue

I am the true vine, and My Father is the vinedresser. Every branch in Me that does not bear fruit He takes away, and every branch that does bear fruit He prunes, that it may bear more fruit. Already you are clean because of the word that I have spoken to you. Abide in Me, and I in you. As the branch cannot bear fruit by itself, unless it abides in the vine, neither can you, unless you abide in Me. I am the vine; you are the branches. Whoever abides in Me and I in him, he it is that bears much fruit, for apart from Me you can do nothing. If anyone does not abide in Me he is thrown away like a branch and withers; and the branches are gathered, thrown into the fire, and burned. If you abide in Me, and My words abide in you, ask whatever you wish, and it will be done for you. By this My Father is glorified, that you bear much fruit and so prove to be My disciples. John 15:1–8

Let the word of Christ dwell in you richly, teaching and admonishing one another in all wisdom, singing psalms and hymns and spiritual songs, with thankfulness in your hearts to God. And whatever you do, in word or deed, do everything in the name of the Lord Jesus, giving thanks to God the Father through Him. Colossians 3:16–17

Table of Contents

God's Secret Revealed

Would you like to discover the secret of how to live with passion for Christ in your personal life, your family, your neighborhood, your church, your community, your place of work, and your world? Would you like to live for Christ not only in the moment of each day's challenges and opportunities but also with consistency over a lifetime of hills and valleys?

If so, do you recognize the human impossibility of those godly desires in this twenty-first-century world, where powerful forces seek to mock Christ and destroy His Church or at least to marginalize both Christ and His Church by ignoring them? Do you realistically grasp the daily war within yourself as saint and sinner?

No self-help book can teach you how to live with passion for Christ! No simple four-step process or eight rules for passionate living give you all the answers you need to succeed. Only God can unlock the secret of how to live with passion for Christ. Paul writes about his ministry "to make the word of God fully known, the mystery hidden for ages and generations but now revealed to His saints. To them God chose to make known how great among the Gentiles are the riches of the glory of this mystery, which is Christ in you, the hope of glory" (Colossians 1:25b–27).

The apostle Paul writes these words humbly and passionately. Paul never forgot how he lived with an ungodly passion as a persecutor of believers in Christ; hence his humility. Christ revealed

God's secret to him on the Damascus road and commissioned him as a servant and a witness to Jews and Gentiles alike. Forgiven by the blood of Christ shed on the cross, Paul lived from then on with passion from God, pure grace: "For this I toil, struggling with all His energy that He powerfully works within me" (Colossians 1:29).

This book's title—*Heartbeat!*—provides imagery for daily and lifelong living with passion for Christ. Physically, you live only because your heart beats twenty-four hours a day, every day, as long as you live. The heart continually pumps blood to all parts of the body and helps the returning blood be cleansed in the lungs and sent out again. Truly, life is in the blood. Physically, God created your heart to beat every moment and throughout your lifespan. Heartbeat!

Spiritually, God's heart beats from eternity with a passionate love for the world and for you. His heart beats in the birth, life, death, and resurrection of His only Son, Jesus, who brought forgiveness of sins, life, and salvation. God's heart beats through His Church, gathered around His Word and Sacraments. His heart beats in you through Baptism as you immerse yourself in the Word of Christ. Consequently, your heart will beat with God's passion for the world as you praise Him, serve others, and bear witness to your faith in Christ daily and throughout your life. Heartbeat!

This Christ-help book intends to let the Word of Christ speak to your heart through the stories of God's people in the Bible and in today's world so that you may be encouraged and strengthened to live with passion for Christ daily and throughout your life. Expect many sections of Scripture to be quoted in this book. Let the Word of Christ speak for itself.

First, we seek godly passion in our lives through the example of God's people. Then, we face squarely the reality that we often pursue passions that drain our energy and lead to bondage. God will lead us to confess those ungodly passions and receive His forgiveness. We will then discover the Word of Christ in new ways, learn to live deeply in that Word, and finally be led by God's Spirit to live God's passion for the world with new eyes and willing hearts. Now God's secret unfolds as the *Heartbeat!* adventure begins.

PART ONE

SEEKING GODLY PASSION IN OUR LIVES

> And they devoted themselves to the apostles' teaching and fellowship, to the breaking of bread and the prayers. And awe came upon every soul. . . . And the Lord added to their number day by day those who were being saved. (Acts 2:42–43a, 47b)

When we seek godly passion in our lives, we often look to others who seem to model that passion for Christ in their lives. The heart of the early community of believers after Pentecost beat with God's heartbeat. This community of faith demonstrated the power of God's Spirit in their devotion to the Word of Christ, their regular reception of Christ's body and blood, prayer together in a spirit of unity, and care for one another. Other people noticed and joined the fellowship as believers in Christ. In addition to biblical examples, we also observe others in our lives who show passion for Christ in their daily lives of witness and service. This section for our growth and understanding tells stories of specific people and groups who live uniquely in the Word of Christ, demonstrating a godly passion and beating with the heartbeat of God's saving love.

Watching People with Passion

A St. Louis-based Christian physician discovered a pressing need to support professional church workers and their spouses struggling with physical, spiritual, and emotional exhaustion as they give their lives to others. As a result, he started a new ministry called Grace Place Lutheran Retreats in order to bring balance and refreshment and help center in Christ their public ministry and personal pilgrim journey. Ultimately, he gave up his medical practice to devote himself full-time to this ministry, helping hundreds of professional church workers and many more in their churches. By God's grace through Christ, good health encourages vibrancy and longevity in family and ministry life—abundant living. Dr. John Eckrich and his wife, Kathy, live with passion for Christ.

A Christian businessman challenges people in midlife to reflect on their first half, like a sports team meeting together at intermission, and to seek God's direction for significant mission in the second half of their life. He candidly describes his first half. As participant and then CEO of a family television business in his 20s, 30s, and early 40s, he achieved great financial success. Although a Christian believer intent on serving the Lord in family, work, and church, he realized that he was mostly driven by a burning desire for success and was in danger of addiction to success. After honest confession to God and prayerful consideration of his future in the light of God's Word as well as counsel from Christian friends, he built on his organizational skills to create Leadership Network, an organization for Christian leaders. Bob Buford lives with passion for Christ.

An older couple without much formal education became part of an outreach ministry at a church I once served. He brought his wife repeatedly to marriage retreats led by my wife and me so she could play the piano—by ear, her special gift—as part of an evening social hour. They both joined a group to make regular home calls on prospective members. In one such visit, because he had once worked in a stable, he was able to relate with empathy and share his faith with a couple grieving the accidental death of a beloved horse. Norma and Byron Raber lived with passion for Christ.

God powerfully used a man named Carl to witness to his family and friends through a pocket cross. Father of a large family, working for many years on the railroad, Carl did not attend church often during his younger years. In retirement, he became much more involved in serving as a church board leader, encouraging his family to join him in worship and demonstrating a growing prayer life. One year, the congregation distributed pocket crosses as part of Lenten worship. Carl proudly carried that cross and showed it to many people, pointing to his Savior and theirs. When he died suddenly not long afterward, his family insisted that the pocket cross be placed in his casket as a witness to his faith in Jesus. Carl lived and died with passion for Christ.

A young servant girl from Israel, taken captive by the Syrian army, served the wife of Naaman, commander of the king's army. He was a valiant soldier, but he had leprosy. We don't even know her name, but she had the courage and caring to speak to her mistress, "Would that my lord were with the prophet who is in Samaria! He would cure him of his leprosy" (2 Kings 5:3). Ultimately, because of her witness, Naaman traveled to Samaria, was healed by the prophet Elisha, and said, "Behold, I know that there is no God in all the earth but in Israel" (2 Kings 5:15). This young servant girl lived with godly passion.

God chose an unknown believer named Ananias in the Church at Damascus to go to the house of Judas on Straight Street and ask for a man from Tarsus named Saul. Saul had just been converted on the Damascus road from an aggressive persecutor of Christians to a believer in Jesus Christ as Savior. Blinded and fasting, he was awaiting further instructions from the Lord. God had chosen this unknown Ananias for a world-changing errand: "Go, for he is a chosen instrument of Mine to carry My name before the Gentiles and kings and the children of Israel" (Acts 9:15). Although he was afraid for his life because of Saul's reputation and authority from the chief priests in Jerusalem, Ananias nevertheless went to Saul, laid hands on him to restore his sight, baptized him, and sent him on his worldwide mission. In that moment, Ananias lived with passion for Christ.

Exploring these six examples of people with passion, we find our hearts stirred by the Spirit's work in others. We want that passion in our own life.

Wanting That Passion for Christ, Now and in the Long Term

> Now when they saw the boldness of Peter
> and John, and perceived that they were
> uneducated, common men, they were
> astonished. And they recognized that
> they had been with Jesus. (Acts 4:13)

Even the enemies of Jesus—in this case, the priests, the captain of the temple, and the Sadducees who brought Peter and John before the Jewish council—are forced to recognize that these uneducated, common men lived with passion for Christ. They had healed a lame man at the temple gate and were now, as prisoners, speaking boldly that this man was healed only by the name of Jesus Christ of Nazareth, crucified and risen, who is the only source of salvation. Astonished, they recognized that Peter and John had been with Jesus.

When we, who by God's grace in our Baptism believe in Jesus Christ as our Savior, hear biblical and contemporary stories of people living with passion for Christ, we want that passion in our own lives. God's Spirit works that desire deep within us. The six brief stories in the previous chapter cause us to consider other examples of believers of our acquaintance or knowledge who live with passion for Christ. You might want to make a short list of people who come to mind. What might we learn for our own daily life?

Think a little more deeply about the six stories and the additional stories on your list. Some of the stories demonstrate passion for Christ in a single moment of opportunity: for example, Byron Raber listening with empathy to a couple grieving the death of a horse or the slave girl from Israel directing Naaman to Elisha. Others display years of more consistent passion for Christ through a God-given venture, such as Dr. John Eckrich's Grace Place Lutheran Retreats, Bob Buford's Christian Leadership Network, or the apostle Paul's mission to the Gentiles. How might God help you live with passion now in the moment? How might God enable you to live with passion for Christ in the long term and with more consistency?

Note also that the six stories introduce different kinds of people with unique backgrounds and personalities, living their faith in different arenas of service. Some are more local and less visible; others are more national or international and more visible. This book does not focus on the external scope of living with passion for Christ, accomplishing goals based on God-given gifts. Kurt Senske's book *The Calling: Live a Life of Significance* (Concordia Publishing House, 2010) addresses those issues very effectively. In contrast, this book, *Heartbeat!,* unlocks the secret of how God's Spirit supplies an unlimited source of daily and long-term passion for Christ through the powerful Word of Christ.

I suspect that none of the people whose stories are recounted in the last chapter would feel comfortable having their stories told as examples of living with passion for Christ. Nor would they consider what they did in the moment or over a period of time as particularly noteworthy. They would rejoice to know that Jesus

Christ was lifted up through their lives and ministries. They are also fully aware of their failures and shortcomings in trying to live with passion for Christ. They depend on God's forgiveness through Christ's death as well as on His daily guidance through His Word for their ventures of service and witness. Would you find that also to be true of the people whom you admire? How might Christian humility hold a key to your own desire to live with passion for Christ, now and in the long term? You see, our physical hearts beat steadily, bringing life to our bodies without our awareness. Spiritually, God's heart beats with our hearts in the moment and in the long term, often without our awareness.

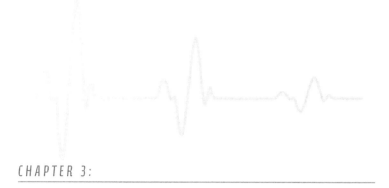

Lord, Give Me a Thirst for Your Word!

Come, everyone who thirsts,
come to the waters.
Isaiah 55:1

As a young pastor who had recently graduated from rigorous theological studies at a seminary, I wanted to live with passion for Christ. I worked very hard at preparing sermons and Bible studies, using all the language tools I had learned. I tried to teach Scriptural doctrines clearly and faithfully for youth and adults alike. I advocated programs that would help people grow in their faith and reach out to others. I attempted to bring God's Word to people sick in hospitals, confined to their homes, facing crisis situations, or dealing with the death of a loved one. Sounds laudable, doesn't it? However, I was often tense, driven, and exhausted. Notice how nearly every sentence in this paragraph begins with the pronoun *I*.

Without doubt, God had made me His child in Baptism. He freely gave me faith in His Son, Jesus Christ, as Savior. He nurtured my faith over the years through Christian parents, pastors, and teachers. He also had called me to serve as a pastor in the Church, and He placed in my heart a desire to serve. Too often, I tried to live with passion for Christ on my own power, and I used the Word of God only as a professional tool for my pastoral ministry.

Gradually, through other Christian friends, God helped me face some of these realities about my own life and service. When a group of young people came to our church to work with our teenagers for a week, God opened my eyes to the power of His Word at work in people's lives. These young people eagerly read and studied God's Word with the freshness of the morning news and prayed openly and naturally. Many lives were touched by their witness, including my own.

As a result, I was led to pray a simple prayer that has transformed my ministry over the years: "Lord, give me a thirst for Your Word! Amen." God answered the prayer immediately by leading me to daily reading and reflection on His Word. That thirst for His Word revitalized my preaching and teaching, my pastoral care and outreach. In the long term, that thirst for the Word of Christ opened my eyes to God's love at work in all of life's circumstances and challenges. The more He teaches me, the more I need and desire to learn. That simple prayer more than forty years ago continues each day.

"Lord, give me a thirst for Your Word! Amen."

Isaiah states an invitation to Israel with similar simplicity and power: "Come, everyone who thirsts, come to the waters" (Isaiah 55:1). Describing salvation as God's free gift "without money and without price" based on His everlasting covenant promised to David, he goes on to describe God's Word, which goes out from His mouth and will not return empty but will achieve the purpose for which He sent it, even as the rain and snow water the earth and make it bud and flourish (Isaiah 55: 10–11).

In Revelation 21, Jesus says, "I am the Alpha and the Omega, the beginning and the end. To the thirsty I will give from the spring of the water of life without payment" (Revelation 21:6). Although salvation is free to us, we know we were redeemed at great cost "with the precious blood of Christ, like that of a lamb without blemish or spot" (1 Peter 1:19).

The more I thirst for the Word of God as a sinner in need of repentance, the more that Word brings me Jesus as Savior, crucified and risen. He enables me to drink from the water of life. The more I thirst for the Word of God, the more He works in me a desire to share the Word of Christ with others who are thirsty for salvation. As you continue to seek godly passion in your life, I invite you to join me in that simple prayer: "Lord, give me a thirst for Your Word! Amen."

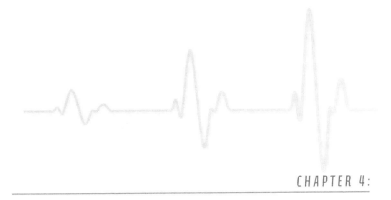

"Could We Have a Couples' Bible Study Group?"

They received the word with all eagerness,
examining the Scriptures daily to see if these
things were so. Many of them therefore
believed, with not a few Greek women of
high standing as well as men.
(Acts 17:11–12)

In January 2004, on a Tuesday evening, two couples showed
up unannounced at a long-established in-depth Bible study
program called LifeLight. For almost fifteen years, members of
our church had been studying individual books of the Bible in a
format that included daily student homework of a study guide,
weekly small-group discussion of that homework by men's and
women's groups, and a weekly lecture by Dr. Erwin Kolb, a noted
church leader belonging to our congregation. Similar groups
met also on Wednesday mornings. As part-time staff and at
Dr. Kolb's request, I had just assumed leadership of the Tuesday
evening program, which was studying the Old Testament Book
of Daniel.

The two couples, Michael and Pat, Bob and Debby, posed a simple question for which I was unprepared: "Could we have a couples'

Bible study group?" They had just completed an adult inquirers' class with the senior pastor and had been received into membership. They were filled with questions about the faith and wanted to dig into God's Word to find answers. They wanted to know more about Christ as their Savior, and they wanted to apply God's Word to their family life and daily lives. For the most part, they had never studied the Bible and came from different religious backgrounds. And they wanted to study together as couples.

These two couples were very much like the Berean Christians described in Acts 17. When Paul came to them on his second missionary journey to teach about Jesus Christ, crucified and risen as their only Savior in fulfillment of the Old Testament Scriptures, these Bereans "received the word with all eagerness, examining the Scriptures daily to see if these things were so" (Acts 17:11).

Their request did not fit the long-established format of classes for LifeLight, but I sensed their genuine desire for growth in Christ. Why not form a couples' group along with the men's and women's groups on Tuesday? I agreed to begin a couples' group in the spring trimester studying 1 and 2 Peter, invited my wife, Gail, to join the group, and arranged to facilitate in addition to providing a lecture for the entire LifeLight group. A new LifeLight community was born.

David and Kati joined that 1 and 2 Peter study. We discovered not only amazing similarities in backgrounds and a common eagerness to study Scripture but also an initial struggle to adapt to the in-depth format of LifeLight. Honest sharing, candid questions, and real-life application characterized our time together, and fervent prayer requests for other family members, friends, and coworkers became a treasured part of our weekly gatherings.

The number of couples in our group doubled in the fall from four to eight as we began studies on the life of David, selected psalms, and Ephesians with 1 and 2 Thessalonians in the 2004–2005 year. The additional couples had been members of our church for a longer period of time but also came from different religious backgrounds and represented different levels of Bible study experience. The opportunity for a husband and wife to learn together as a couple seemed important in every case.

Without attempting to overemphasize numbers of participants, the group grew to a high of sixteen couples; as we complete our eighth year together, it has rounded out at ten couples. In that eight-year span, God has provided an amazing variety of couples and individuals for brief or longer time periods—engaged couples, friends for whom we had been praying appearing to thank us for our prayers, younger and recently married couples who came for a year or two before starting their family and therefore not being able to continue. Some left the group because of major leadership responsibility in our congregation, new Bible study ventures in their homes, or other reasons. Members have forged ongoing relationships because of time together around the Word of Christ. Group members have gathered in support of weddings, anniversaries, birthdays, Baptisms, and funerals.

New members of our group have provided depth of insight, vitality for our fellowship, and prayer for people needing faith in Christ. Informal gatherings at our home and at those of others, in the spring, late summer, and Christmastime, help us focus on Christ, His Word, and personal mission opportunities in our lives. Through formal study and informal communication, God leads us to confess our struggles and sins honestly, rejoice in His forgiveness through Christ's death, welcome new insights from His Word, and seek new ways to serve Him. The room often fills with laughter, poignant silence, and overflowing thanksgiving to God. Over these eight years, the group has also studied John, miracles, Genesis and Revelation, Exodus and Hebrews, Matthew and Minor Prophets, Acts and Proverbs, and a just-concluded overwhelming sixty-six-chapter study of Isaiah. All of this richness came from a simple question: "Could we have a couples' Bible study group?"

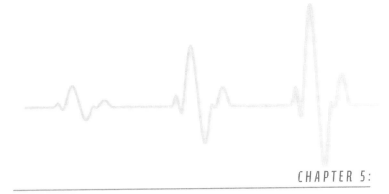

Observing
Senior Saints

O God, from my youth You have taught me,
and I still proclaim Your wondrous deeds.
So even to old age and gray hairs, O God, do
not forsake me, until I proclaim Your might
to another generation, Your power to all those
to come. Psalm 71:17–18

We can seek godly passion in our lives by observing the Spirit's lifelong work in senior saints through the Word of Christ. David's words in Psalm 71, written near the end of his life, testify to God's saving actions in his lifespan.

One senior saint whose lifelong mission stands out in my mind is my former colleague and mentor, who died in 2002 at the age of 97. A former district president in The Lutheran Church—Missouri Synod and longtime pastor of St. Paul Lutheran Church, Decatur, Illinois, Dr. Alvin W. Mueller continued in his mission during his long years of retirement—preaching, teaching, and influencing children, grandchildren, and great-grandchildren in his seventy-two years of marriage. His wife, Eleanor, likewise provided a shining example of grace and caring for so many. When I last saw him in an assisted living facility two months before his death, he was still interested in the mission efforts of the Church at large and encouraging the residents of his home for the elderly to attend worship services there. At his funeral, which I attended, his widow, other family members, former church members, and many church leaders gave testimony to his faithful witness to Jesus Christ as the only way to salvation. Thank God for Dr. Mueller's passion for Christ!

When I served as pastor at St. John Lutheran Church, Peru, Indiana, I was privileged to know a senior saint named Minnie Krieg and to officiate at her funeral. Minnie lived alone in an apartment. A shut-in with one leg amputated, Minnie never complained but was alive in Christ and intent on the Church's worldwide mission. She supported many international ministries and cared deeply about her local congregation. I kept her abreast of our outreach to the community, and she willingly served as a prayer warrior. I will always remember her intelligent eyes and ready smile. Minnie's mature witness to Jesus and powerful prayer life resulted from a lifetime of God's faithful teaching. Thank God for Minnie Krieg's example of living in the Word of Christ!

The Wednesday morning men's Bible study group, which I lead as part of the LifeLight ministry, builds my own faith in Christ and my love for God's Word in a powerful way. These men have years of experience in the realities of life, much practical wisdom, penetrating questions, and a love for digging into Scripture humbly and expectantly. They rejoice to see Christ revealed in Scripture and insist on practical application to their lives and a better understanding of today's world. Earl, a class member in his nineties, regularly lifts up fervent prayer for our church body and our nation and beseeches God for us to be better soul winners and soul keepers every day.

Thank God for these senior saints gathered around God's Word!

In the early verses of Psalm 71, written by David probably in his old age, he remembers God's faithful protection since birth and gives bold witness to his rock and his hope: "My mouth is filled with Your praise, and with Your glory all the day" (verse 8). David goes on to look beyond his own problems and accusers to affirm his hope in God and his determination to tell of God's salvation all day long. Then he declares in his old age: "O God, from my youth You have taught me, and I still proclaim Your wondrous deeds" (verse 17).

God had indeed taught David a great deal. He chose him as the Lord's anointed, gave him victory over the giant Goliath, protected him from Saul's efforts to take his life, preserved him from the Philistines and other enemy nations, made him king first of Judah and then of all Israel, convicted him of his adulterous relationship with Bathsheba and his murder of Uriah, and then forgave his sin through the prophet Nathan. God also helped David deal with all of his family problems that resulted from his earlier sin, restored him as king after Absalom's rebellion, and fulfilled His promise to continue David's reign through David's greater Son, Jesus the Messiah. No wonder David bears witness in old age to God's marvelous deeds!

You saw how the Word of Christ fills senior saints such as David, Dr. Alvin Mueller, Minnie Krieg, and a Wednesday men's Bible class with a passion to live for Christ. What senior saints inspire you to believe in the Savior and to share His message with others?

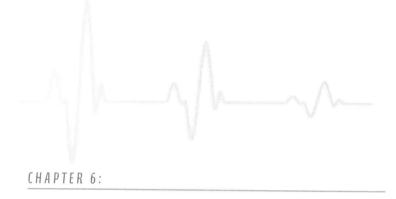

"What More Is There to Say but *Amen*?"

> Amen! Blessing and glory and wisdom and
> thanksgiving and honor and power and
> might be to our God forever and ever! Amen.
> (Revelation 7:12)

This chapter tells the story of one man, captive to the saving message of Jesus Christ. His passionate love for the Word of Christ spilled over into his life of laughter and self-effacing outreach to others. Dr. Oswald C. J. Hoffmann, former radio speaker for *The Lutheran Hour* from 1955 to 1988, classical linguist, and influential church worker worldwide, touched the lives of countless thousands with his clear proclamation of faith in Jesus Christ as the only way to salvation.

One personal anecdote reveals the man behind the message. Concordia Publishing House published Dr. Hoffmann's autobiography, *What More Is There to Say but Amen,* in 1996. As president of Concordia, I invited him and his wife, Marcia, to have lunch with my wife, Gail, and me in my office in order to thank him for his writing. Before lunch, he was to sign books in our bookstore and provide a radio interview. When we went down to greet him, we were shocked to see his head swathed in a bandage attached around his chin like a bonnet. Shortly before, Dr. Hoffmann fell outside his home and had been treated at a hospital for a large hematoma. Completely unself-conscious about his appearance, he was giving the interview, autographing books, and vigorously shaking hands with people all the way to the elevator leading up to my office. Our lunch was totally relaxed as he told stories about hiring Gail's father as a teacher at Concordia College—New York, and reaching out to our family. His wife, Marcia, was more concerned than he was about his health and need for rest.

"A WORD FROM THE AMEN CORNER"

In 2005, I attended a memorial service for Dr. Hoffmann. After preaching at length from Scripture about the wonders of God's plan of salvation for sinful human beings, he would often conclude, "What more is there to say but *amen?*" At this memorial service, therefore, Pastor Vern Gundermann used the theme "A Word from the Amen Corner," with Revelation 7:12 as his text.

At Dr. Hoffmann's Baptism in 1913, as well as at his confirmation, his ordination, and in the many aspects of his worldwide ministry, believers in the amen corner were constantly saying amen to God's grace, mercy, and forgiveness through the death and resurrection of Jesus Christ. I remember, for example, listening to him teach at a pastors' conference in northern Indiana many years ago. He held a Greek New Testament in his hand and read to us with his own translation directly from the original language.

Now, at this memorial service with organ, brass, and the Bach Society Chorus, in Scripture readings and proclamation, we were lifting our voices to say once again, "Amen! Yes, it shall be so!" Our eyes were lifted to that scene described in Revelation 7: a great multitude from every nation, tribe, people, and language standing before the throne and in front of the Lamb, wearing white robes and holding palm branches. What will they say? "Salvation belongs to our God who sits on the throne, and to the Lamb!" (Revelation 7:10), followed by angelic praise from the amen corner: "Amen! Blessing and glory and wisdom and thanksgiving and honor and power and might be to our God forever and ever! Amen" (Revelation 7:12).

I don't know about you, but I am moved by the life and proclamation of Dr. Hoffmann to keep the amen going while I have breath, so that many may join those multitudes at the throne singing amen forever. Luther's explanation of the Conclusion of the Lord's Prayer includes a similar *amen:* "For Thine is the kingdom and the power and the glory forever and ever. Amen. What does this mean? This means that I should be certain that these petitions are pleasing to our Father in heaven and are heard by Him. . . . Amen, amen means 'yes, yes, it shall be so' " (Luther's Small Catechism, Lord's Prayer, Conclusion).

GALATIANS 2:20

> I have been crucified with Christ. It is no
> longer I who live, but Christ who lives in me.
> And the life I now live in the flesh I live by
> faith in the Son of God, who loved me and
> gave Himself for me. (Galatians 2:20)

When Dr. Hoffmann autographed my copy of *What More Is There to Say but Amen,* he referenced Galatians 2:20. That passage characterized his life and ministry.

In this epistle, St. Paul has been forcefully chiding the Galatians for departing from faith in Jesus to rely again on the works of the Law for their salvation. He repeats the truth, "We know that a person is not justified by works of the law but through faith in Jesus Christ" (Galatians 2:16a). Christ *for* us on Calvary. Christ *in* us through our Baptism, where we daily die to sin and live to righteousness. All by faith. All by God's grace for Christ's sake.

That message was Dr. Hoffmann's theme every week on *The Lutheran Hour* and in every one-on-one and group encounter. In his first broadcast, he said, "I want you to know that our only purpose in these broadcasts is to share—and to share—and again to share—Jesus Christ with you." Galatians 2:20 gives us all the power we need to live with passion for Christ and provides the message as well: "faith in the Son of God who loved me and gave Himself for me." Thank God for the singular focus of Oswald Hoffmann on the Gospel of Jesus Christ for today's world!

TRIBUTE TO MARCIA

> He who finds a wife finds a good thing and
> obtains favor from the Lord. (Proverbs 18:22)

When Dr. Hoffmann wrote his 1996 autobiography, he paid tribute to his wife, Marcia. In 2000, she preceded him in death after sixty years of marriage. After the funeral, I looked him right in the eye and told him how sorry I was for his loss. He replied with a tear in his eye, "I miss her so much!"

His stirring words in his tribute to her reveal how God uses each of us to testify to Jesus Christ in our lives: "To Marcia with love—art student in Minneapolis and promising dress designer who married a struggling preacher; mother of four strapping children, and their educator in the perennial absence of the same struggling preacher; anonymous contributor to one good cause after another; discerner of the spirits with a clear eye focused on the Gospel; bearer of the burning torch of Christ the Savior to anyone who has ever met her" (Hoffmann, 5).

How tenderly the book of Proverbs describes a godly wife: "He who finds a wife finds a good thing and obtains favor from the LORD" (Proverbs 18:22). In Proverbs 31, the wife of a noble character has these traits: "She opens her mouth with wisdom. . . . Her children rise up and call her blessed; her husband also, and he praises her: . . . A woman who fears the LORD is to be praised" (Proverbs 31:26, 28, 30). Marcia Hoffmann obviously was a godly person toward her husband, her family, and the many people she met worldwide as she traveled with him and supported his ministry. God's favor in Jesus' death and resurrection came through Marcia to many.

How do you bear "the burning torch of Christ the Savior" to everyone you meet? What special and creative gifts has God given you for service and witness? What opportunities is God presenting you in your home and through your home to many others? How does God's favor, first freely bestowed on you as an undeserving sinner, pass through you to others? Thanks be to God for Oswald and Marcia Hoffmann.

"A BLAZING SENSE OF HUMOR"

The cheerful of heart has a continual feast.
(Proverbs 15:15b)

Dr. Paul Maier, son of the first speaker of *The Lutheran Hour,* writes comments about Oswald Hoffmann in the first part of *What More Is There to Say but Amen:* "He always had—and has—a blazing sense of humor that is only augmented when his own laughter takes on a 'second wind' and a merely funny joke becomes hilarious" (Hoffmann, p. 11). Dr. Hoffmann, who was free in Christ and enthused about the Gospel and who loved to relate with people, displayed "a blazing sense of humor." His hearty laughter was contagious.

How well the words of Proverbs describe his life: "The cheerful of heart has a continual feast" (15:15). In the same chapter, "A glad heart makes a cheerful face" (verse 13). "To make an apt answer is a joy to a man, and a word in season, how good it is"! (verse 23). "The light of the eyes rejoices the heart, and good news refreshes the bones" (verse 30).

To be sure, Oswald Hoffmann knew the depth of human depravity, including his own sin. He knew the reality of war and the pain of human suffering. He also knew the joyful Good News of God's salvation through Jesus Christ, who shouldered our sins on the cross and won the victory over Satan. He knew God's grace, which brings us to faith in Christ, and His sure promise of abundant life now and life forever in heaven.

That gave him reason for joy and laughter: "The cheerful of heart has a continual feast." He laughed at *The Lutheran Hour* rallies, pastoral conferences, private homes, on fishing trips, and at the annual Schlachtfest in Frankenmuth, Michigan, where sausage is made.

All because of the Gospel of Jesus Christ! The Gospel is contagious. Let that "blazing sense of humor" spread.

AROUND THE WORLD

> As You sent Me into the world, so I have sent
> them into the world. (John 17:18)

The funeral of Dr. Oswald Hoffmann gave us opportunity to reflect on the impact of his life and ministry worldwide. His joy and zeal for the Gospel of Jesus Christ led him to travel extensively to Europe, Africa, and the Far East and to visit with presidents and kings: Dwight Eisenhower, John F. Kennedy, Lyndon Johnson, Richard Nixon, Norway's King Olaf, Haile Selassie of Ethiopia, and the King of Tonga. He also visited the troops in Vietnam. He served as honorary president of the United Bible Societies and participated in national and international evangelism congresses as well as the Second Vatican Council. His joyful faith and consistent focus on Christ as Savior as revealed in Scripture touched many lives worldwide.

In His High Priestly Prayer, Jesus prays for His disciples: "As You sent Me into the world, so I have sent them into the world" (John 17:18). He wants them to have His "joy fulfilled in themselves" (verse 13) and the truth of God's Word so that they will be able to witness powerfully and effectively. His prayer is answered after Pentecost, when the believers go out with bold testimony and courageous actions in the face of persecution, imprisonment, and death.

Recognizing our own fearfulness and flagging zeal, we claim Christ's forgiveness and the full measure of His joy. Dr. Hoffmann's amen to God's love in Christ inspires us to live with passion for Christ as He sends us into the world. Amen to God's heartbeat in Dr. Hoffmann's life and ministry!

Learning across Cultures

But as for you, continue in what you have
learned and have firmly believed, knowing
from whom you learned it. (2 Timothy 3:14)

All too often, our understanding of living with passion for Christ and our appreciation for the Word of Christ is narrowly limited by our own cultural context in North America and our local church experience. My own perspective on God's saving work through Christ and the power of His Word has been greatly broadened by getting to meet and learn from Christian believers in a variety of cultures throughout the world. This chapter lifts up the stories of people living with passion for Christ and treasuring God's unfailing Word worldwide.

A STALWART SAINT FROM SLOVAKIA

In early 1992, shortly after many countries in Eastern Europe had been liberated from Soviet control, I was privileged to travel to Slovakia. There I met the bishop of the Lutheran Church in Slovakia, Pavel Uhorskai. His steadfast faith in Jesus Christ and his life of suffering inspired me then and continues to shape my witness today.

As a young pastor with an evangelistic outreach to youth, he clashed with the Communist government because of his continuing proclamation of Christ as Savior. He spent time in prison and was then forced to work as a common laborer in the construction industry for years, denied the opportunity to serve as a pastor. After the fall of Communism, he was chosen by the Lutheran Church in Slovakia to serve as their bishop. At the age of 70, he was serving with a clear focus on the Gospel, demonstrating a wisdom and kindness tempered by his years of suffering for the faith.

My time in his presence reminded me of Paul's witness to Timothy from prison based on his "teaching, [his] conduct, [his] aim in life, [his] faith, [his] patience, [his] love, [his] steadfastness, [his] persecutions and sufferings" (2 Timothy 3:10–11). Paul's charge to Timothy reminds me of my meetings with Bishop Uhorskai and equally applies to you as you daily reach out in mission to those around you: "But as for you, continue in what you have learned, . . . knowing from whom you learned it and how from childhood you have been acquainted with the sacred writings, which are able to make you wise for salvation through faith in Christ Jesus" (2 Timothy 3:14–15).

TREASURING GOD'S WORD IN CHINA

On a trip to China in 2000, I was privileged to meet Pastor Bao, the man in charge of supervising the printing of Bibles by Amity Press. At the time, this was the only place that the Chinese government permitted Bibles to be produced. In the course of working with him and his staff and inviting his family to have dinner with us at our hotel, I found him to be a man of deep faith who treasured the Word of Christ and wanted to make it available throughout his country. He described the courage of his father, who consistently shared his faith in Christ while riding trains in China, even though he risked his life by doing so.

Pastor Bao was preparing a calendar for Christians in China. He told us that his father was selecting Bible verses for each calendar day, praying on his knees for the Spirit's help in his selection process. He also gave us a limited-edition print of the story of the prodigal son by a Chinese Christian artist. I learned a great deal from Pastor Bao about how precious God's Word is, especially since the Bible was not permitted to be printed or read in China for years.

A DACHA CONVERSATION

> Therefore, as you received Christ Jesus the
> Lord, so walk in Him, rooted and built up
> in Him and established in the faith, just as
> you were taught, abounding in thanksgiving.
> (Colossians 2:6–7)

St. Paul's words to the Colossians remind me of a visit to Russia, where we were welcomed at the dacha, or country home, of Fyodor and Natasha, a few miles outside of Moscow. We had never met them before, but we were treated graciously with a tour of the surrounding countryside, including a small village Orthodox church and a historical museum, as well as a hike through fields and a hilly wooded area near a river. Seated around the table in their dacha, we ate delicious food from their garden and engaged in meaningful conversation.

To our joy, we learned that these highly educated scientists, at one time prominent in the Soviet nuclear program, shared our faith in the triune God. Their parents and grandparents had experienced persecution for their faith. The Church was an integral part of their lives, and they had arranged for their grandson to be baptized. Their deeply rooted faith in Christ Jesus as Lord expresses itself in their caring lives and thankfulness for God's gifts, including the wonders of His creation in the Russian countryside.

Paul's words to the Colossians in the first chapter describe our ongoing communication with Fyodor and Natasha: "In the whole world [this Gospel] is bearing fruit and growing—as it also does among you, since the day you heard it and understood the grace of God in truth" (Colossians 1:6).

Our faith in Christ was strengthened as a result of our dacha visit. We shared God's grace at work in our lives in America and gave thanks with them for His saving presence in Russia. We need each other around the world to tell the story of Jesus and His love.

A BAPTISMAL
TESTIMONY

> Repent and be baptized every one of you in
> the name of Jesus Christ for the forgiveness of
> your sins. (Acts 2:38)

Ran Xu, a PhD student at the University of Nebraska, gave a testimony on the day of her Baptism that makes Acts 2 come alive in our hearts for witnessing to the world:

> Back in mainland China, I didn't have many opportunities to know who Jesus really was. After I came to the U.S., in order to make friends and to improve my English, I went to University Lutheran Chapel. Just like a kid in school, I was curious about the Bible, but I didn't pay much attention to it.
>
> As I became more involved in activities and met more Christians, I began to wonder: "What drives Christians to cook for those homeless people, to give money to the Chinese baby who needs eye surgery,

and to help build houses destroyed by a storm?" Eventually, I attended more Bible studies and had more conversations with other Christians. I began to realize it is not human ability but the power of God's Word that guides Christians to give their lives to others.

According to the Bible, we are all sinners, and the wages of sin is death. We all need repentance and forgiveness. We are saved from our own death because Jesus died in our place. God not only gave us His Son. He also gave us the Holy Spirit. We know what it means to be loved by God, so we can return love and serve others.

My Baptism is a result of two very happy years of learning God's Word, receiving love from other Christians, examining my own life, and repenting of my own sin. As a new Christian, I really need to strengthen my faith. I am also more excited to share my faith with non-Christians. I will let God's Word guide my life, no matter what happens.

SEEKING
AND FINDING

That they should seek God, in the hope that they might feel their way toward Him and find Him. Yet He is actually not far from each one of us. (Acts 17:27)

In his famous sermon in Athens on Mars Hill, St. Paul pointed to an altar marked "To the unknown God" and told the Athenians about the God of creation, who made every nation of the earth to live in a certain place and in a certain time so that man would seek Him and find Him, though He is "not far from each one of us." This

God sent Jesus to die for the world's sin and to rise from the grave. Today, many are brought to faith in Jesus as they travel around the world. Here is the story of one Iranian man now living in St. Louis.

Ten years ago, in his mid-twenties, this man was living in Tehran, Iran, and like all Iranians considered himself Muslim. Nevertheless, he felt like he was looking for God. The more he thought about it, the more he felt everything was wrong with Islam. He read the Koran and found that the more he read, the more questions he had. He wasn't happy. Life was dark; there was no harmony. Yet somewhere he felt a small light in his heart—a hope.

Afraid of possible persecution in Iran, he moved with his family to Germany, where a Christian aunt invited him to go to church with her. For the first time, he felt that he could find the answers to his spiritual questions. Listening each week while his aunt held a Bible study in her home, he began to read the Bible with interest. He wanted a change in his life and believed in Jesus as God. In Christianity, he found the ultimate truth. Now in St. Louis, he wants to be a lifelong student of the Bible and a missionary to those that need to know Jesus, especially all of the people in Iran. He is very grateful to God for the gift of his Christian faith.

Has God touched your heart through these stories from Slovakia, China, Russia, and Iran? These Christian believers, often finding themselves in hostile environments, have turned to the Word of Christ to help them live with passion for Christ as they continue to learn about Him. I have learned a great deal from them. God's heart beats around the world in the lives of believers.

Walking in the Footsteps
of Martin Luther

In September 2010, Gail and I hosted a tour to the Luther lands in Germany. After years of reading, learning, and teaching the Reformation message of faith alone, grace alone, Scripture alone, Christ alone, we were actually walking in the footsteps of Dr. Martin Luther. A spiritual giant in the sixteenth century, Luther continues to provide a stellar example of the theme for this book, *Heartbeat!*. We visited Eisleben, where he was born on November 10, 1483, and baptized the next day in the Church of St. Peter and St. Paul; Eisenach, where he went to school; and Erfurt, where he received his university degrees and entered the Augustinian monastery. These towns and medieval buildings gave us a sense of Luther's life and piety as he grew and struggled with a just God who punishes sinners and the unjust. However, Martin Luther's story of grace-filled faith in Christ and courageous confession of that faith can best be told in three locations—Wittenberg, Worms, and the Wartburg Castle.

My heart leaped for joy as I walked in Martin Luther's footsteps down the main street of Wittenberg from the Augustinian monastery, which later became his parsonage, past Melanchthon's house and the city center with its town church, St. Mary, where Luther served as preaching pastor, to the Castle Church at the other end,

HEARTBEAT!: Living with Passion in the Word of Christ

the university church with its door used as a "bulletin board" for academic theses. Here Luther lived, wrote, preached, and taught as the Reformation exploded throughout Europe.

In the tower room of the Augustinian monastery (today called Luther House), Luther's study of the Bible triggered the Gospel insight that started the Reformation. He wrote as follows:

> To be sure, I was unusually zealous in trying to understand Paul in his Epistle to the Romans. . . . Even though I was living as a blameless monk, I felt that before God I was still a sinner with an uneasy conscience. I could not rely on being justified by making my own amends. I was not able to love this "just" God. In fact, I hated Him because He punishes sinners. . . . This caused me to rage, driven by a wild and confused conscience. I ruthlessly kept on beating my head against that particular passage of Paul's. I was hungry and thirsty to find out what St. Paul was trying to say.

> Finally, God showed me mercy. After racking my brains for days, I suddenly noticed the correlation of the words in the verse: "For in it the righteousness of God is revealed from faith for faith, as it is written, 'The righteous shall live by faith' " (Romans 1:17). At that point, I began to understand the righteousness of God: namely, that the person who is justified because of a gift of God lives by it and, in fact, by faith. At that point, I felt like I had stepped through an open gate into paradise. Suddenly, all of Scripture opened itself up to me seamlessly in a brand-new light. I ran through Scripture by memory and discovered the same concept in other passages: God's work consists in what He works in us. God's power consists in His

making us powerful. God's wisdom consists in His making us wise. The same is true for the strength of God, the salvation of God, and the honor of God. Now, as much as I used to hate the righteousness of God, I now lifted up this sweetest of words in my love. In this way, this passage of Paul became the gate to paradise for me. (*Traveling with Martin Luther,* pp. 34, 36.)

Luther was the product of his era and had the Church's teaching drummed into his heart and mind. He needed to live counter culture in order to discover God's justification by God's grace for Christ's sake through faith. His superior, Johann von Staupitz, assigned him to preach and teach the Bible at the new university in Wittenberg. Luther plunged into a study of the Scriptures in their original languages of Greek and Hebrew—preparing lectures on Genesis, the psalms, and Paul's Letters to the Romans and Galatians. God spoke through His Word to bring Luther the life-changing insight from Romans 1:17 referenced above. He was able to live with passion for Christ in the turbulent years ahead of him because God revealed to him the Holy Scriptures as the Word of Christ and His righteousness.

Visiting the Castle Church at the other end of Wittenberg's main thoroughfare called to mind Luther's Ninety-five Theses. Intended only as academic theses for a better understanding of indulgences, these published theses caused a firestorm in the Church, which led to a papal condemnation of Luther and his writings. Based on his study of the Scriptures and the clear teaching that "the entire life of a believer should be one of repentance" (Ninety-five Theses, thesis 1), this document, posted on October 31, 1517, led Luther to a deeper study of the Bible as he debated and wrote additional treatises in response to attacks from all over the Church.

WORMS: A COURAGEOUS CONFESSION OF FAITH

Although our tour did not include the city of Worms, this city figures prominently in the Reformation. On April 16, 1521, the small town of seven thousand was full of visitors because Luther had been ordered to appear before Emperor Charles V and the Imperial Diet to recant his writings. Given one additional night to consider his answer, he reappeared before the council on the afternoon of April 18 and, when compelled to give a yes or no answer, spoke these words: "Unless I am convinced by the testimony of Scripture and clear reasoning (for I trust neither the pope nor councils alone, since it is well-known that they have often erred and contradicted themselves), my conscience is bound to the passages in Holy Scripture I have cited. I am held captive by the Word of God. Hence, I cannot and will not retract anything, because it is neither safe nor salutary to go against conscience" (quoted in Cornelia Dömer, *Traveling with Martin Luther,* p. 82). As a result of his stand on the Word of Christ, Luther was declared an outlaw of the empire by Charles V.

WARTBURG CASTLE: THE NEW TESTAMENT TRANSLATED FOR THE PEOPLE

On the outskirts of Eisenach, we climbed to the towering medieval Wartburg Castle. At the end of the castle tour, we visited Luther's study, where he translated the New Testament into idiomatic German based on the original Greek. Rescued from the emperor by friends of the Elector, Frederick the Wise, he was a virtual prisoner for several months for his own safety. In the preface of that "September Testament," he wrote, "So, too, the Gospel of God and the New Testament resonated from the apostles into the whole world as the Good News and as a proclamation of victory by the true David who battled with sin, death, and the devil and overcame them. And in so doing, He redeemed, justified, made alive, and saved all who had been held captive in sin, plagued by death, and overwhelmed by the devil—even though they had not merited their salvation" (quoted in *Traveling with Martin Luther,* p. 85).

Fresh from that Luther land tour, I realized in a new way that we walk in the footsteps of Martin Luther when we live counter culture and immerse ourselves in the Word of God, which reveals Christ our Savior again and again. We can live with passion in that Word of Christ. God's heart beats strongly through His Church.

ALIVE WITH THE HEARTBEAT OF THE REFORMATION

All . . . are justified by His grace as a gift,
through the redemption that is in Christ Jesus.
(Romans 3:23–24)

How vital is our beating heart! We often take for granted how the heart assures circulation of fresh blood. When problems arise, we realize how very important the heart is to the body.

The heartbeat of the Reformation is the teaching of justification by God's grace for Christ's sake through faith. This vital teaching provides fresh life for the Church at all times. When it predominates, a healthy Church worships, obeys, serves, and grows. When it is neglected, the very existence of the Church is threatened.

The Early Church had heart problems. Paul's opponents held up the Law as the means to salvation. This teaching led either to self-righteousness or to despair. Paul writes about this in Romans 3. The sixteenth-century Church also had heart problems. The Church recommended doing penance, buying indulgences, and venerating relics as ways to earn salvation. Once again, people became either self-righteous or despairing. Then Martin Luther spoke out boldly. Today's Church faces heart problems too, whenever we make the Law a means of justification before God. If we think our giving, serving, witnessing, and church involvement will justify us, we grow either self-righteous or despairing. The Church develops sluggish blood, grows tired and breathless.

Paul renews the Church with the ringing affirmation of Romans 3:23–24. We stand before the Judge. Are we guilty or innocent? The evidence of our sins against the Law cries out for a guilty verdict, but God looks to the sacrifice of His sinless Son on Calvary and declares us righteous, not guilty. He gives us faith in Christ's death and resurrection, and as a result, we are justified by grace. Our spiritual heart beats strong, and we serve Him. The Church's heart beats strong, and the Gospel sounds forth to the world.

CHAPTER 9

Making the Bible Yours

My good friend Jackie Oesch lives with passion in the Word of Christ. Wife of a pastor and mother of four, she desires to connect people to Jesus through Bible studies that teach Bible stories. Very active for years in Christian women's ministries, she worked side by side with her husband in the Pastoral Leadership Institute, which he founded, concentrating on supporting pastors' spouses in the Institute and helping develop them as leaders in the home, the Church, the community, and the world. Through Full Value Ministries, a not-for-profit Christian organization that she founded, she now provides Bible studies beginning with a course called "Making the Bible Yours," which provides navigational tools for students who have little experience with the Bible but have a desire to study on their own.

In the beginning of "Making the Bible Yours," Jackie encourages new students with these words: "You are embarking on a new adventure that will shape the rest of your life. This Bible study is designed with you in mind. Your journey will be unique to you and will be determined in part by your eager and enthusiastic passion to grow in your understanding of the Book, the Bible. Your commitment to the study promises to enrich your life as God speaks through His Word to you" (Jackie Oesch, *Making the Bible Yours,* p. 5).

Her passion for sharing Bible studies that teach Bible stories causes her to spend hours and days in the writing process. As of this moment, ten courses are available that have been developed since 2007, and the remaining courses will be completed by 2012 or 2013. Some courses are already available in Chinese, Korean, Swahili, Spanish, and Portuguese. God is blessing Jackie's humble but determined efforts to introduce many to the Word of Christ so that they may live with passion for Christ.

SEEKING GODLY PASSION IN OUR LIVES

This first section of the book has told many stories of people with passion for Christ. Some are well-known, like Martin Luther and Oswald Hoffmann, while others are unknown to most: people from various walks of life, such as laborers, physicians, and businessmen and women, and from diverse cultures, such as China, Slovakia, Iran, and Russia. As a result, we seek godly passion for our lives now and in the long term with the knowledge that we often fall short. All the people of passion whose stories we have told—whether biblical or contemporary—have also fallen short because of sin and have also relied on the Word of God to connect them to Jesus, their Savior and their righteousness. Desiring passion for Christ, we now face the reality of pursuing passions that drain our energies and passions that lead to bondage. We have heart problems.

PART TWO

PURSUING PASSIONS THAT
DRAIN AND LEAD TO BONDAGE

Part one of this book radiated hope and promise. We watched people living lives filled with passion for Christ. God's Word pointed them to Christ for their salvation and moved them to reach out to others in unique ways, at times of opportunity and over an extended period of time. Their stories inspire us to seek godly passion in our lives.

Part two brings a chilling reality factor to our search. Anyone beginning a journey, planning a project, or undertaking a business needs to count the cost. We can evaluate our prospects of success by identifying driving and restraining forces. Driving forces encourage us to move forward. They could include our desire to reach the goal, education and experience, adequate financial resources, willing and capable people to join us, and a genuine need and enthusiasm for the goal to be reached.

Restraining forces include everything that might stand in the way of our goals: weakness on our part in terms of energy, stamina, ability, or financial resources, possible obstacles such as a faltering economy, fierce competition, the wrong goal, the wrong timing, or unfavorable public opinion. Any decision to move ahead with confidence and expectation requires a clear-eyed grasp of driving and restraining forces.

Jesus challenges the crowds traveling with Him to count the cost of being a disciple:

> Whoever does not bear his own cross and come after Me cannot be My disciple. For which of you,

desiring to build a tower, does not first sit down and count the cost, whether he has enough to complete it? Otherwise, when he has laid a foundation and is not able to finish, all who see it begin to mock him, saying, "This man began to build and was not able to finish." Or what king, going out to encounter another king in war, will not sit down first and deliberate whether he is able with ten thousand to meet him who comes against him with twenty thousand? And if not, while the other is yet a great way off, he sends a delegation and asks for terms of peace. So therefore, any one of you who does not renounce all that he has cannot be My disciple. (Luke 14:27–33)

This part of the book forces us to consider restraining forces in this twenty-first-century world, forces that threaten our desire to seek godly passion in our life. These threats come both from outside—the world—and from inside: our own sinful flesh. Satan drives both the world and our sinful selves to pursue passions that drain and passions that lead to bondage. God wants us to understand the enemy fully so that we might place our reliance totally on Him for the daily and lifelong *Heartbeat!* adventure of living with passion in the Word of Christ. Are you ready to face spiritual warfare in the twenty-first century?

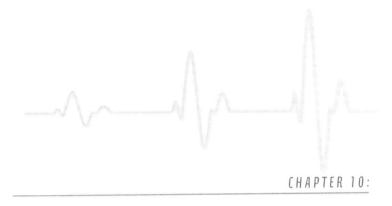

CHAPTER 10

Conflicting Passions

For I know that nothing good dwells in me,
that is, in my flesh. For I have the desire to do
what is right, but not the ability to carry it out.
For I do not do the good I want, but the evil I
do not want is what I keep on doing. Now if I
do what I do not want, it is no longer I who do
it, but sin that dwells within me.
(Romans 7:18–21)

The following chapters will face head-on the temptations of our world. Short-term and long-term worldly pursuits lay claim on our lives in specific ways to drain our energies and lead us into bondage. However, the starting point for spiritual warfare is the war within. Paul describes it so poignantly in the verses from Romans 7 quoted above. Fully aware that the wages of sin is death for Jews and Gentiles alike, Paul rejoices that "the free gift of God is eternal life in Christ Jesus our Lord" (Romans 6:23). Yet he recognizes a daily struggle between the crucified and risen Christ, within us in our Baptism, and our sinful flesh, which leads us to do evil and not good.

Martin Luther describes this inner warfare as the reality that we are at the same time saint and sinner: 100 percent saint because we wear the robe of Christ's righteousness won for us by His death and resurrection, and 100 percent sinner because of our flesh. No wonder we are tempted to pursue worldly passions that drain and lead us to bondage. Yet we are covered by Christ's righteousness.

For our comfort as we face ungodly pursuits, Paul brings realistic Gospel hope:

> For I delight in the law of God, in my inner being, but I see in my members another law waging war against the law of my mind and making me captive to the law of sin that dwells in my members. Wretched man that I am! Who will deliver me from this body of death? Thanks be to God through Jesus Christ our Lord! (Romans 7:22–25)

Earlier, Paul had written these words:

> For the death He died He died to sin, once for all, but the life He lives He lives to God. So you also must consider yourselves dead to sin and alive to God in Christ Jesus. (Romans 6:10–11)

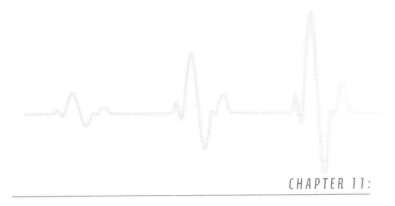

The Drain of Time Pressures and High-Tech Overload

Look carefully then how you walk, not as
unwise but as wise, making the best use of
the time, because the days are evil.
(Ephesians 5:15–16)

Images of fast-paced life in our twenty-first-century world flash before our eyes. Cars whiz by on crowded interstates. Impatient shoppers line up at check-out lanes, where harried clerks scan barcodes and generate credit or debit card receipts. Smartphones yield news, weather, and time and generate text messages and replies while their users converse, shop for groceries, or fill the car with gasoline. Work-generated e-mails pile up; another Internet conference awaits. Family members go their separate ways, with school projects, sporting events, jobs, social events, and church activities all competing for attention, scheduling, communication, and transportation. Social networks, computer games, recorded television programs, and live television sporting events dominate the remaining time minus sleep and meals. Do time pressures and high-tech overload drain your passion for Christ?

ONE DAY

So teach us to number our days that we may
get a heart of wisdom. (Psalm 90:12)

Monday morning dawns as the alarm jars you awake. The all-too-brief and yet exhausting weekend is over, and the rat race begins again. Yesterday's worship helped you a great deal to taste and see that the Lord is good. The Scripture readings, hymns, and sermon struck home with the Good News of Christ. Confession of sins along with the assurance of forgiveness in Absolution and Holy Communion brought further comfort. Family time and conversation with Christian friends enriched your day.

With resolve to begin your day and week in the Lord, you get out of bed, exercise, shower, sit down to breakfast, and spend a few moments in devotion and prayer with the family. However, you and they feel rushed to get ready and face the day. You all head in separate directions to work and school. Your head begins to pound as you drive through traffic and try to figure out your day.

Demands crowd in immediately as you arrive at work: projects to schedule, problems to solve, e-mail messages to answer, meetings to attend, deadlines to meet, ruffled feelings to smooth over. Too much coffee puts you on edge. Energy levels drop when the caffeine wears off. You sprint from one task to another when the day calls for a marathon pace. You rush lunch at your desk, plow through the afternoon and can't wait to head home. The drive home, with errands to run and children to pick up from school and after-school activities, leads to a rushed supper and an evening with more responsibilities. Collapsing into bed at a late hour, you pray for help from your heavenly Father to sleep and face another day. Do time pressures and high-tech overload drain your passion for Christ?

ONE MONTH

My times are in Your hand; rescue me from the
hand of my enemies and from my persecutors!
(Psalm 31:15)

Look back over the last month. How did your plan for it to go?
What events filled your calendar? How many of those activities
were required? Where did family time receive attention? What
time did you schedule for church attendance and Bible study? How
much leisure time was allotted?

How do you feel about the month now? How would you change
your schedule? What went wrong? What unexpected time pres-
sure crowded out important things? What activities kept you from
reaching out to others in your family, work, church, and community? In what ways did circumstances lead you astray and drain
your passion for Christ? When did you give in to your sinful flesh
to waste time, crowd your time, or pursue wrong uses of your time?

How will you plan the new month? What different plans will
you make? What activities are absolutely required? What time do
you want to reserve for important activities neglected last month?
What additional time do you want to reserve for personal prayer
and the study of God's Word as well as for group spiritual growth?
What activities will you avoid or minimalize? How will you maximize time for service and witness?

You have just asked yourself twenty questions about how to
live one month of time. The psalmist's prayer for rescue from enemies is based on his powerful statement of trust in God's salvation
through the Messiah, Jesus: "My times are in Your hand" (Psalm
31:15).

ONE YEAR

Make us glad . . . for as many years
as we have seen evil. (Psalm 90:15b)

In these days of time pressures and high-tech overload, Satan conspires with our sinful flesh and the world's crazed agenda to drain us of our passion for Christ and our immersion in the Word of Christ. We uncover that conspiracy when we examine a single day of our life and ask questions about how we spend one month of our time. Perhaps we can discover more and plan better when we concentrate on one year of our life.

On New Year's Eve, many people review the previous year, thanking God for His many blessings and confessing their many failures. Then they look ahead to the New Year, with or without resolutions to change their behavior and priorities. Whether or not you are reading this book as a new calendar year begins, you can look at one year beginning today from the perspective of dealing with time pressures and high-tech overload.

First, admit the problem. No matter what we do or refuse to do with our minutes and days, the time pressures will continue. Economic problems such as job loss and a housing crisis create greater time pressures for desperate people. The continuing rapid advance of technology almost forces people to adapt, learn new technologies, and rush to keep up with the time demands created by constant communication, tighter deadlines, and less leisure time. Because of our sinful flesh and the world's agenda, time pressures and high-tech overload will drain our passion for Christ to some extent.

Second, see the new year as a year of God's grace. Pray with the psalmist, "Make us glad . . . for as many years as we have seen evil" (Psalm 90:15b). The year ahead of us offers endless promise and possibilities because the same God who walked with us last year leads us into the new with the assurance of salvation through Christ, the promise of His presence in the Word of Christ, and the commission to bring Christ through our lives to the world. We will need His forgiveness and guidance daily. Because our times are in His hands, we can face the problem with a fresh commitment to use both time and technology in His service. Each new year provides new opportunity for change and adjustments of our time so that we may live with passion in the Word of Christ.

> Behold, now is the favorable time; behold, now
> is the day of salvation. (2 Corinthians 6:2)

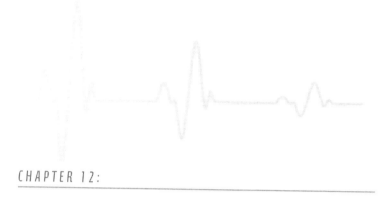

The Drain of Just Surviving

Be gracious to me, O Lord, for I am
languishing; heal me, O Lord, for my bones
are troubled. My soul also is greatly troubled.
. . . I am weary with my moaning; every night I
flood my bed with tears. (Psalm 6:2–3, 6)

Last night, our entire metropolitan area was ravaged by a fierce
storm of rain, hail, straight-line winds over sixty miles per hour,
and at least three tornadoes. We knew that it was coming and
that it would arrive while we were sleeping. Just after we went to
bed and fell asleep, the tornado sirens began to blare. First, the
radio issued the warning. Constant lightning flashed. Grabbing
robes and a flashlight, we headed for the basement. We turned
on local television news to discover the meteorologists operating
on generator power, fearing for their own safety, and showing a
blotchy radar screen of the storm line passing through the entire
area. Scattered reports came through of tornadoes sighted and
damage suspected, some close to our home.

Now awake but very tired, we watched television for about an
hour with eyes glued to the screen. Then when the savage storm
moved across the Mississippi River into Illinois, we trudged back
to bed and tried to go back to sleep, wondering if an additional
storm from the southwest was headed our way. This morning, we

dragged ourselves out of bed, made coffee, and watched the local news report the extent of the widespread damage from more than 150 storm reports and three tornadoes in the metropolitan area. Yet we had survived with no apparent damage.

This storm danger was cumulative. Like most of the nation, our area had experienced a very active winter storm pattern—many snow and ice storms and a devastating rash of tornadoes on New Year's Eve, which had left homeless some members of our local church. On that occasion, my wife and I experienced lock down in a local shopping mall, separated in different stores for over an hour until the all-clear was sounded. Although safe in every storm event, we felt the drain of just surviving.

Through so many circumstances of life in our twenty-first-century world, Satan drains our energies for living with passion for Christ by creating in us the frequent feeling that we are just surviving. The psalmist so many years ago describes a similar despair. He refers to physical, emotional, and even spiritual problems that raise survival anxiety: "My bones are troubled. . . . My soul also is greatly troubled. . . . I am weary with my moaning; every night I flood my bed with tears" (Psalm 6:2–3, 6). He brings his fearful feelings to the Lord for forgiveness, healing, and deliverance: "O LORD, rebuke me not. . . . Be gracious to me, O LORD; . . . heal me, O LORD. . . . Turn, O LORD, deliver my life" (Psalm 6:1–2, 4). He concludes, "The LORD has heard my plea; the LORD accepts my prayer" (Psalm 6:9).

Honestly looking at our turbulent emotions, we discover that all too often we feel drained even when we are outwardly safe. Daily demands overwhelm. Conflicts within our family, church, and work environment sap our energy. Physical problems such as lack of sleep, poor eating habits, lack of exercise, and chronic aches and pains discourage and distract us from service to others. Too much focus on ourselves and our daily anxieties makes us feel that we are just barely keeping our heads above water. We may also be gripped with spiritual guilt and emptiness, making us feel cut off from God. Satan rejoices, the world scoffs, and our sinful flesh makes us wallow in the daily and cumulative drain of just surviving.

The Word of Christ leads us outside of ourselves to see a saving God and people in need of our service and witness. Just listen to these comforting and challenging words from the psalms:

> I love You, O LORD, my strength. The LORD is my rock and my fortress and my deliverer, my God, my rock, in whom I take refuge, my shield, and the horn of my salvation, my stronghold. I call upon the LORD, who is worthy to be praised, and I am saved from my enemies. (Psalm 18:1–3)

> Turn to me and be gracious to me, for I am lonely and afflicted. The troubles of my heart are enlarged; bring me out of my distresses. Consider my affliction and my trouble, and forgive all my sins. (Psalm 25:16–18)

> The LORD is my light and my salvation; whom shall I fear? The LORD is the stronghold of my life; of whom shall I be afraid? (Psalm 27:1)

> Trust in the LORD, and do good; dwell in the land and befriend faithfulness. Delight yourself in the LORD, and He will give you the desires of your heart. Commit your way to the LORD; trust in Him, and He will act. (Psalm 37:3–5)

> I waited patiently for the LORD; He inclined to me and heard my cry. . . . He put a new song in my

mouth, a song of praise to our God. . . . Blessed is the man who makes the LORD His trust. . . . "I delight to do Your will, O my God; Your law is within my heart." I have told the glad news of deliverance in the great congregation. (Psalm 40:1, 3–4, 8–9)

Because of the devil, the world, and our sinful flesh, we will continue at times to experience the drain of just surviving. God brings salvation through His Son, who was forsaken by everyone including His heavenly Father but who won victory on the cross. He brings us forgiveness and strength from His Word to praise His name and reach out to others in our life. We move from just surviving to overcoming.

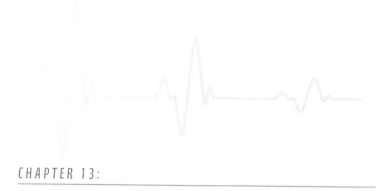

The Drain of a World out of Control

> Desolation is left in the city; the gates are battered into ruins. For thus it shall be in the midst of the earth among the nations. (Isaiah 24:12–13)

This chapter describes the external drain of a world out of control, in contrast to the internal drain of feeling that we are just surviving, which was covered in Chapter 12. Evidence abounds. On the world scene, terrorism strikes unexpectedly and violently, causing senseless loss of life and destruction of property. Drug cartels gain power, work across national boundaries, kill any person or group standing in their way, and bring untold suffering, misery, and death to addicted users in the urban, suburban, and rural areas of our country and others. War rages against terrorist strongholds in many parts of the world. Radical Islamic fundamentalists assume power in nations and prey on other nations to advance their cause. The Middle East and Africa often explode with protests to overthrow dictators of one persuasion or another, causing instability and the danger of restricting oil supplies or commerce on the seas.

In our own nation, rising debt, a failed housing market, catastrophic job losses, and shaky local, state, and national governments facing insolvency create a world out of control for average Americans. Violence increases in our cities, with drive-by shootings and armed robbery appearing often in the daily news. Protests increase and tempers flare as competing groups try to deal with these massive problems. Leadership often looks weak, wrongheaded, or self-serving.

How do you respond to a world out of control? Do you spend hours watching or reading bad news, helpless to do anything about it? Do you hide your head in the sand, going about your busy days trying to keep safe and make ends meet? Do you seek involvement to make things better by joining a political movement or contributing in some way to solve problems in your place of work or community? Are you searching God's Word for understanding, strength, and direction? How are you praying about a world seemingly out of control? Do these realities drain your energy or energize you to live with passion for Christ?

God speaks through the prophet Isaiah to reveal His coming judgment against a rebellious world: "Desolation is left in the city; the gates are battered into ruins. For thus it shall be in the midst of the earth among the nations" (Isaiah 24:12–13). In chapters 24–27, Isaiah summarizes chapters 13–23, in which he speaks against the rebellious nations of that historical period, such as Babylon, Egypt, Moab, and Assyria, as well as against His own people in Jerusalem. God now addresses all nations of all times, which will be destroyed in the final judgment when Christ comes again. Isaiah continues:

> On that day the LORD will punish the host of heaven,
> in heaven, and the kings of the earth, on the earth.
> They will be gathered together as prisoners in a pit;
> they will be shut up in a prison, and after many days

they will be punished. (Isaiah 24:21–22)

No longer need we be drained by a world seemingly out of control when we realize that God is in total control. He is bringing us to the final judgment, when all believers in Christ will welcome the reigning Messiah to the heavenly Mount Zion. Isaiah writes, "On this mountain the LORD of hosts will make for all peoples a feast of rich food, a feast of well-aged wine. . . . He will swallow up death forever; and the Lord GOD will wipe away tears from all faces, and the reproach of His people He will take away from all the earth, for the LORD has spoken" (Isaiah 25:6, 8).

How then do we respond to the disturbing drain of a world seemingly out of control? Realities will persist. The world is a mess, internationally and domestically. Why? Jesus prays to the Father in His High Priestly Prayer: "I have given them Your word, and the world has hated them because they are not of the world, just as I am not of the world." (John 17:14 NIV). In this verse, John uses *world* to describe the human system opposed to God's purposes. The Father's beautiful world, created to serve and praise Him, has been shattered by the ugliness of sin. Satan, the prince of this world, conspires to destroy God's created world by sowing seeds of disobedience and rebellion. That human system includes terrorists, drug lords and pushers, egomaniacal dictators, corrupt politicians, drive-by shooters, self-serving protesters, greedy bankers, and attention-grabbing media people. However, by nature we are the children of wrath even as these others are, and we can all too easily be sucked into this evil human system. The Holy Spirit, the Counselor, convicts the world of guilt in regard to sin and condemns the prince of this world (John 16:7–11). We confess our own sin in the face of a sinful world out of control. There is absolutely no room for compromise with the sinful world.

Only the death of Jesus on the cross atones for the sins of the world. As His baptized children through faith in His saving Word, we are set free from this sinful world system led by Satan. We are set free to search His Word for strength and guidance, set free to pray for our troubled world, issue by issue and person by person, set free to warn unbelievers of the consequences of their disobedience and to point them to Jesus' blood and righteousness, set free to involve ourselves regularly as Christian citizens in many down-to-earth ways, and set free to long for Christ's coming again with arms of love for all believers. Once again, only the Word of Christ can supply the passion we need for joyful living in this world.

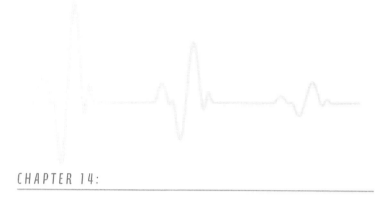

The Drain of Church Letdowns

> I therefore, a prisoner for the Lord, urge you
> to walk in a manner worthy of the calling to
> which you have been called, with all humility
> and gentleness, with patience, bearing with one
> another in love, eager to maintain the unity of
> the Spirit in the bond of peace.
> (Ephesians 4:1–3)

We strongly seek godly passion in our lives, encouraged by the Word of Christ and inspired by the stories of people living with passion for Christ. When we face the debilitating drain of time pressures and high-tech overload, the internal, sinking feeling of just surviving and the external vortex of a world out of control, that godly passion to live for Christ seems to be slipping away.

Weary and battered, we turn to the Church for help and reenergizing. We long for that Church fellowship after Pentecost described in Acts 2:42–47. We believe Paul's incredible words about Christ's Church in Ephesians 2, bridging the humanly impossible gap between sinners dead in trespasses and a holy God and between alienated Gentiles and circumcised Jews:

> "So then you are no longer strangers and aliens, but
> you are fellow citizens with the saints and members

of the household of God, built on the foundation of the apostles and prophets, Christ Jesus Himself being the cornerstone, in whom the whole structure, being joined together, grows into a holy temple in the Lord. In Him you also are being built together into a dwelling place for God by the Spirit" (Ephesians 2:19–22).

How wonderful God's Church sounds! We seek refreshment and rest, encouragement and revitalization to live with passion for Christ in this twenty-first-century world. Then, all too often, our godly passion is further depleted by the drain of church letdowns.

Picture these images of realities in the institutional church in our day at local, regional, and denominational levels. Local churches find their numbers dwindling. Few young people and children sit in the pews. Strapped for financial resources to pay salaries and keep the doors open, the local church constantly asks for more contributions. Members quarrel with one another over issues of church maintenance, social events, and fund-raising projects. Visitors feel unwelcome as tight-knit circles of family and friends socialize with each other. Pastors and church leaders become adversaries, with the former demanding respect and authority over spiritually ignorant lay leaders and the latter treating their spiritual leaders as hired hands to be controlled and discarded at will.

Culture wars rage in some churches and between churches over style of worship, church architecture, methods of outreach, social action and societal issues, Bible translations, and church discipline. These wars often divide church members at regional and national levels. Important theological issues often lie at the heart of such disagreements, and people of good will seek scriptural guidance for their positions, wanting to be centered in Christ as Savior and to rely on God's Spirit working through Word and Sacraments.

Some churches offer little scriptural teaching, appealing to the lowest common denominator of biblical doctrine, using words and images from the world and pop culture, and emphasizing friendships and low-level commitments. This approach may attract numbers and make people feel good about themselves, but it lacks biblical integrity and a focus on Christ as Savior. People who come burdened by guilt and needing forgiveness may leave empty and discouraged with no Gospel hope and comfort. These images apply across the spectrum of Christianity in North America.

Do you ever experience the drain of church letdowns? You may not currently belong to any church but long for sound teaching from the Word of Christ and a fellowship of believers to help you face the world. Finding a local church may be difficult because of the institutional realities described above. Perhaps you belong to a church that leaves you drained either because of shallow biblical preaching and teaching or because of judgmental lovelessness in the fellowship. Even if God has blessed you with a church fellowship in which the Gospel is preached in its truth and purity, the Sacraments are rightly administered, and love abounds, Satan still is working overtime to undermine that teaching and divide the fellowship.

Just as individuals are at the same time saint and sinner, so Satan works in churches to bring division, unfaithfulness, and lovelessness. In the Book of Revelation, John is instructed to write these words to that same Church in Ephesus: "But I have this against you, that you have abandoned the love you had at first. Remember therefore from where you have fallen; repent, and do the works you did at first" (Revelation 2:4–5). They had abandoned the Word of Christ and therefore love for one another.

For that reason, we rely totally upon God working through the Word of Christ to establish, preserve, and grow His Church on earth. Though human institutions fall far short of God's glory, God's Church continues joyfully and powerfully until Christ comes again.

Although church letdowns also drain our energies, we seek out and fully support God's local expression of His Church, where believers gather around Word and Sacrament so we may mature in our faith and speak God's truth in love to our world. Paul writes to the Ephesian Church:

> And He gave the apostles, the prophets, the evangelists, the shepherds and teachers, to equip the saints for the work of ministry, for building up the body of Christ, until we all attain to the unity of the faith and of the knowledge of the Son of God, to mature manhood, to the measure of the stature of the fullness of Christ, so that we may no longer be children, tossed to and fro by the waves and carried about by every wind of doctrine, by human cunning, by craftiness in deceitful schemes. Rather, speaking the truth in love, we are to grow up in every way into Him who is the head, into Christ. (Ephesians 4:11–15)

How, then, do we respond to the drain of church letdowns? Admitting our own sinful church attitudes and the human failings of both spiritual leaders and church members, we embrace our local church "with all humility and gentleness, with patience, bearing with one another in love, eager to maintain the unity of the Spirit in the bond of peace" (Ephesians 4:2–3). God moves us beyond church letdowns to church passion for "speaking the truth in love" (verse 15).

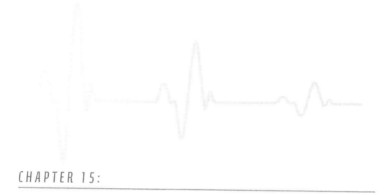

The Bondage
of Materialistic Pursuits

> Give me neither poverty nor riches; feed me
> with the food that is needful for me, lest I be
> full and deny You and say, "Who is the LORD?"
> or lest I be poor and steal and profane the
> name of my God. (Proverbs 30:8–9)

Far worse than passions that drain our energy are worldly passions that lead to bondage. In the next chapters, we confront four of those passions that can destroy our relationship to God and lead us far from the Word of Christ. First, pursuing materialistic gain can seductively entrap us and consume all our energies.

Investment advisors will tell you that the greatest enemies of a growing investment portfolio are greed and fear. When the economy goes well and investments grow at a rapid pace, we want more and more. Blinded to high risks, investors buy speculative stocks on margin and lose great wealth when the economic downturn suddenly accelerates. Greed brings us down. On the other hand, when a depression seems imminent, many investors feel fearful of catastrophic loss and irrationally sell investments at the worst possible time. Fear causes great damage.

Many years ago, a wise person in the book of Proverbs lifted up a powerful prayer about the role of wealth in our relationship with God: "Give me neither poverty nor riches; feed me with the food that is needful for me, lest I be full and deny You and say, 'Who is the LORD?' or lest I be poor and steal and profane the name of my God" (Proverbs 30:8–9). He wanted to rely upon the Lord for daily bread rather than become driven by greed to gain more and more wealth, thus forgetting God, or become filled with fear because of no wealth and resort to stealing, which dishonors God. Greed and fear can both lead to bondage in the pursuit of material things.

Our culture breeds both greed and fear through materialistic pursuits. Lotteries offer millions of dollars for the lucky winner. In pursuit of that prize, millions of people spend more and more of their earnings for that unlikely win. Gambling casinos seduce many others to have fun and win, but few succeed. First, greed dominates, and then fear takes over to mire the loser deeper and deeper in debt.

Advertising in many forms showcases the allure of material possessions: expensive automobiles, jewelry, fashionable clothes, boats and fishing gear, exotic vacations, and luxury homes. Greed can lead to mortgage and credit card debt far beyond our ability to pay. The recent housing market collapse and implosion of the financial industry converted greed into fear for many people on the street. Gradually, we find ourselves hopelessly in bondage. Governments teeter in the balance. Businesses fail. Jobs are lost. Whether in boom or bust times, materialistic pursuits can dominate our lives and leave little room for God or His Word.

Listen to how clearly the Word of God addresses and exposes this bondage in both Old and New Testaments. Through the prophet Isaiah, God condemns the leaders of Judah and the women of Zion with these words:

The LORD will enter into judgment with the elders and princes of His people: "It is you who have devoured the vineyard, the spoil of the poor is in your houses. What do you mean by crushing My people, by grinding the face of the poor?" declares the Lord GOD of hosts. (Isaiah 3:14–15)

The LORD said: Because the daughters of Zion are haughty and walk with outstretched necks, glancing wantonly with their eyes, mincing along as they go, tinkling with their feet. . . . In that day the Lord will take away the finery of the anklets, the headbands, and the crescents; the pendants, the bracelets, and the scarves; the headdresses, the armlets, the sashes, the perfume boxes, and the amulets; the signet rings and nose rings; the festal robes, the mantles, the cloaks, and the handbags; the mirrors, the linen garments, the turbans, and the veils. (Isaiah 3:16, 18–23)

The prophet Amos exposes the materialistic bondage of Israel's leaders:

Woe to those who lie on beds of ivory and stretch themselves out on their couches, and eat lambs from the flock and calves from the midst of the stall, who sing idle songs to the sound of the harp and like David invent for themselves instruments of music, who drink wine in bowls and anoint themselves with the finest oils, but are not grieved over the ruin of Joseph! Therefore they shall now be the first of those who go into exile, and the revelry of those who stretch themselves out shall pass away. (Amos 6:4–7)

Jesus teaches in His Sermon on the Mount:

Do not lay up for yourselves treasures on earth,

where moth and rust destroy and where thieves break in and steal, but lay up for yourselves treasures in heaven. . . . For where your treasure is, there your heart will be also. . . . No one can serve two masters, for either he will hate the one and love the other, or he will be devoted to the one and despise the other. You cannot serve God and money. (Matthew 6:19– 21, 24)

Paul writes the Philippians about living with passion for Christ instead of living in bondage to material pursuits:

Not that I am speaking of being in need, for I have learned in whatever situation I am to be content. I know how to be brought low, and I know how to abound. In any and every circumstance, I have learned the secret of facing plenty and hunger, abundance and need. I can do all things through Him who strengthens me. (Philippians 4:11–13 NIV)

How do materialistic pursuits impact your life right now—as gifts of God used in His service or as growing bondage to Satan, squelching your passion for Christ? God knows your heart and wants an honest answer, with the promise of forgiveness through His Son and a whole new perspective in the Word of Christ, which can help you live with Paul's passion in all circumstances with Christ's strength.

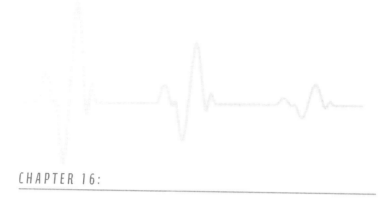

The Bondage of Sexual and Internet Pornography Pursuits

> The body is not meant for sexual immorality, but for the Lord, and the Lord for the body. . . . Shall I then take the members of Christ and make them members of a prostitute? Never! . . . Flee from sexual immorality. (1 Corinthians 6:13, 15, 18)

Sexual sins abound in our culture and often pass as acceptable behavior for consenting adults expressing their natural desires. In fact, "living with passion" often suggests sexual expressions between various partners, casual or committed. Once a year, our community celebrates Mardi Gras as a last fling before Ash Wednesday. The celebration is now the second largest in the country, next to New Orleans, and the cry is "Let the good times roll!" While one can celebrate Mardi Gras in a wholesome manner, enjoying the parade with family and friends, many people drink and carouse to excess. In one establishment, Mardi Gras beads are available with condoms. Satan uses the world's sexual practices to inflame our sinful selves with lust, which can lead to bondage.

Sexual passion between a man and a woman within marriage pleases God as enjoyment of His creation. However, sexual passion outside of marriage opens the floodgates of destructive habits that ultimately destroy our bodies, minds, and spirits. That is why Paul writes to the Corinthian Christians, living in a sexually permissive pagan culture, that "the body is not meant for sexual immorality, but for the Lord" (1 Corinthians 6:13).

Sexual temptations begin with lustful looks filling our thoughts and bodies with lustful urges. Television and movies have used sexually explicit materials to sell products for years. The *Sports Illustrated Swimsuit Issue* illustrates how print media attract attention for profit. Jesus makes clear in His Sermon on the Mount how the commandment against adultery includes lustful looks:

> You have heard that it was said, "You shall not commit adultery." But I say to you that everyone who looks at a woman with lustful intent has already committed adultery with her in his heart. (Matthew 5:27–28)

In our high-tech age, sexual lust has been inflamed with increased intensity through Internet pornography. Web sites abound with explicit pornographic material beyond any standard of decency and can be explored in the privacy of one's room. Millions are becoming addicted to regular viewing. This addiction is bondage, and it requires treatment to overcome. Many believers in Christ, including spiritual leaders, involve themselves in such pornography and try to keep this shadow life hidden from their families, friends, and church members. All too often, this obsession leads to sexual involvement with someone identified on a social network, destroying marriages and family life.

Self-serving sexual passion can prevent and destroy our living with passion for Christ. Should we be surprised by sexual bondage as one of Satan's significant tools? Paul writes to the Roman Christians how God's wrath is revealed against all ungodliness and unrighteousness of men. Their rejection of Him is expressed in idolatry and foolish hearts. That idolatry leads to all manner of sexual lust and perversions: "Therefore God gave them up in the lusts of their hearts to impurity, to the dishonoring of their bodies among themselves" (Romans 1:24).

How do you respond to such deadly sexual temptations so they do not lead you into bondage? First, take them very seriously, heeding Paul's counsel: "Flee from sexual immorality" (1 Corinthians 6:18). Our choices of what we watch and don't watch, read or don't read, Google or don't Google make a huge difference in Satan's or the world's efforts to lead us astray. The same thing applies to our relationships with others, especially of the opposite sex. More time in the Word of Christ and less time with cultural temptations strengthens our minds, bodies, and spirits. As Paul writes to the Ephesians, "For at one time you were darkness, but now you are light in the Lord. . . . Take no part in the unfruitful works of darkness, but instead expose them. For it is shameful even to speak of the things that they do in secret" (Ephesians 5:8, 11–12).

Second, be honest about those sexual temptations that threaten you, and confess your sins immediately when you succumb. Seek consultation with your pastor and confess to him. Receive Christ's full and free forgiveness each time you receive the Lord's Supper as His baptized child. Paul writes, "You were taught, with regard to your former way of life, to put off your old self, which is being corrupted by its deceitful desires; to be made new in the attitude of your minds; and to put on the new self, created to be like God in true righteousness and holiness" (Ephesians 4:22–24 NIV).

Third, use Christ's forgiveness of your sexual sins and the Spirit's empowering through the Word of Christ to increase your godly passion for service and witness to others. You are a walking billboard for God's saving work in your life. John writes:

> For all that is in the world—the desires of the flesh
> and the desires of the eyes and pride in possessions—
> is not from the Father but is from the world. And
> the world is passing away along with its desires, but
> whoever does the will of God abides forever. (1 John
> 2:16–17 NIV)

Paul adds, "Finally, be strong in the Lord and in the strength of His might. Put on the whole armor of God, that you may be able to stand against the schemes of the devil" (Ephesians 6:10–11).

You are a walking billboard because you are a forgiven sinner. God has made you strong with the full armor of His Word, and you are now taking your stand against sexual bondage in His strength. That's living with godly passion.

Paul finishes his discussion of sexual immorality for the Corinthian Christians with these powerful words of Gospel motivation: "Do you not know that your body is a temple of the Holy Spirit within you, whom you have from God? You are not your own, for you were bought with a price. So glorify God in your body" (1 Corinthians 6:19–20).

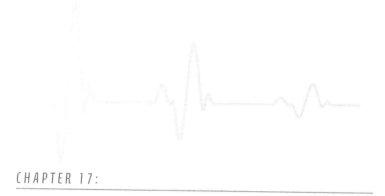

The Bondage of Sports and Leisure Pursuits

Do you not know that in a race all the runners run, but only one receives the prize? So run that you may obtain it. Every athlete exercises self-control in all things. They do it to receive a perishable wreath, but we an imperishable. So I do not run aimlessly; I do not box as one beating the air. But I discipline my body, and keep it under control, lest after preaching to others I myself should be disqualified. (1 Corinthians 9:24–27)

In today's culture, sports and other leisure pursuits dominate our time and attention on many levels. Children are almost forced to participate at an early age by parents, siblings, and peers. Baseball, basketball, soccer, football, track and field events, gymnastics, volleyball, ice hockey, tennis, golf, and swimming seek to engage our youth. Each sport requires large amounts of time, money, skill development, and commitment. Sports can provide healthy development of body, mind, and spirit. Team play can build relationships, determination, and healthy competition with a sense of accomplishment when goals are reached.

In fact, the apostle Paul uses the athletic competition of his day—specifically, the Isthmian Games near Corinth—as a metaphor for the intensity of his Gospel ministry to Jews and Gentiles alike, becoming all things to all people, so that he might save some—all for the sake of the Gospel (1 Corinthians 9:16–23). He encourages the Corinthian Christians to run flat out for the finish line with purpose and to box effectively, not wasting a motion as they share Christ with others (1 Corinthians 9:24–27). He points out, however, that the athletic contests only provide perishable prizes (such as a wreath), while the Gospel race provides an imperishable crown by God's grace for Christ's sake (1 Corinthians 9:25).

Could sports and leisure pursuits, commendable in themselves, lead you and your children on a road to bondage? Did you as a youth overcommit yourself to athletic competition, particularly if you excelled in one or more sports? Did you squeeze out everything else, including relationships, in pursuit of your achievements? What happened when your playing days were over? Did you try to hang on or fall into depression?

As a parent, do you push your children to succeed at all costs, hoping they will fulfill your frustrated dreams for yourself? Do you show poor sportsmanship while rooting for your child's teams by yelling at umpires, referees, coaches, and other players? How do you treat your children when they fail to succeed or drop out of sports activities? In a very subtle manner, our own sports participation or that of our children can lead us on a road to bondage for a perishable crown that fades away.

Now broaden the bondage to include your passion for sports as a spectator. You may have your favorite team and player at the high school, college, or professional level. To what extent do you pursue your passion from season to season, with season tickets, pre- and post-game rallies, multiple sports packages on television,

Internet information and updates, and fan gatherings at sports bars? How much time do you devote to fantasy football or other sports? Again, these pursuits can be either a healthy use of leisure time or lead you to bondage. Our culture devotes enormous and perhaps idolatrous attention to Super Bowl Sunday, March Madness, and playoffs in all sports.

Leisure pursuits add to the question of bondage. The endless pursuit of strong and beautiful bodies spawns whole industries of diets, exercise, tanning booths, apparel, cosmetics, and pop psychology therapies. Our attempts to take care of our God-given bodies can quickly lead to an obsession that keeps us constantly stirred up, guilty, and at the same time proud of our accomplishments.

Leisure entertainment through sporting events, concerts, art fairs, drama and movies, and seasonal events such as Mardi Gras and St. Patrick's Day offer enjoyable time with friends and special food and drink. However, such activities can also lead to excesses that can cause bondage and addictions, fueling the neglect of our daily service to others and of productive work.

The prophet Isaiah speaks against the excesses of Judah, which would lead them to exile:

> Woe to those who rise early in the morning, that they may run after strong drink, who tarry late into the evening as wine inflames them! They have lyre and harp, tambourine and flute and wine at their feasts, but they do not regard the deeds of the LORD, or see the work of his hands. (Isaiah 5:11–12 NIV)

How can you enjoy sports and leisure pursuits without letting them lead you down the road to bondage? First, recognize participation in sports and leisure time, indeed everything in our lives, as gifts of God. The psalmist writes:

> How precious is Your steadfast love, O God! The children of mankind take refuge in the shadow of Your wings. They feast on the abundance of Your house, and You give them drink from the river of Your delights. (Psalm 36:7–8)

> Delight yourself in the LORD, and He will give you the desires of your heart. (Psalm 37:4)

> It is good to give thanks to the LORD, to sing praises to Your name, O Most High; to declare Your steadfast love in the morning, and Your faithfulness by night, to the music of the lute and the harp, to the melody of the lyre. For You, O LORD, have made me glad by Your work. (Psalm 92:1–4)

Next, confess your excessive pursuit of sports and leisure activities. Be specific and honest as the Spirit guides your thoughts. Claim Christ's forgiveness and blessing of your leisure time. Rejoice in the Gospel words of the psalmist as you run Christ's race for an imperishable crown:

> Bless the LORD, O my soul, and forget not all His benefits, who forgives all your iniquity, who heals all your diseases, who redeems your life from the pit, who crowns you with steadfast love and mercy, who satisfies you with good so that your youth is renewed like the eagle's. (Psalm 103:2–5)

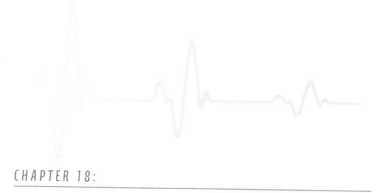

The Bondage of False Spiritual Pursuits

> You shall have no other gods before Me. You shall not make for yourself a carved image, or any likeness of anything that is in heaven above, or that is on the earth beneath, or that is in the water under the earth. You shall not bow down to them or serve them; for I the LORD your God am a jealous God. (Deuteronomy 5:7–9)

This twenty-first-century world teems with idolatrous religions, misleading philosophies, self-help remedies, satanic cults, and mix-and-match spiritual approaches. Many people believe in the so-called spiritual realm of gods and goddesses, witchcraft and demons. They explore Eastern religions, Islam, Scientology, New Age religion, nature goddesses, crystals, cosmic convergence, beings from outer space—and the list goes on and on. They often blend in various parts of the Christian faith as having some spiritual meaning. It is politically correct to show tolerance toward all of these spiritual pursuits, and therefore it is dangerous to make exclusive claims about one God, the Father of our Lord Jesus Christ, the only Savior of the world through His death and resurrection. Likewise, the world scoffs at the belief that only

God's revelation of Himself through the Word of Christ by the power of the Holy Spirit can lead to saving faith.

Therefore, Satan tempts us to join the world in these false spiritual pursuits, initially in small ways as we read an interesting spiritual novel, listen to a competent and persuasive talk show host or speaker, hear about remarkable miracles or seemingly transformed lives on YouTube, or get to know someone who seems likeable and credible but relies on a totally different god than we do. Before we realize what is happening, that false spiritual pursuit leads us deeper and deeper into bondage. Stories abound of Christians being drawn into cults and losing all sense of reality as they believe the cultic leader and adapt their total daily lives to a strict order. Witchcraft, Satanism, and the occult lead to similar bondage.

Nothing has changed regarding spiritual bondage. When Adam and Eve desired to be like God instead of remaining joyfully content as His creatures, the spiritual bondage began. The tower of Babel gave witness to the same idolatry. In His love, God chose a special people, beginning with Abraham, and brought them by grace out of slavery in Egypt to Mount Sinai, where He gave them the chief commandment: "You shall have no other gods before Me" (Deuteronomy 5:7). They responded with continual idolatry, starting with a golden calf and then embracing the gods of Canaan. Many pursued this spiritual bondage. God warned them before they entered Canaan:

> There shall not be found among you anyone who burns his son or his daughter as an offering, anyone who practices divination or tells fortunes or interprets omens, or a sorcerer or a charmer or a medium or a necromancer or one who inquires of the dead, for whoever does these things is an abomination to the LORD. (Deuteronomy 18:10–12a)

The Israelites did not heed the warning. After centuries of idolatry and before Judah's defeat and captivity in Babylon, God warned them again through the prophet Isaiah:

> "Is there a God besides Me? There is no Rock; I know not any." All who fashion idols are nothing, and the things they delight in do not profit. Their witnesses neither see nor know, that they may be put to shame. (Isaiah 44:8b–9)

Nothing had changed in the New Testament world either, when the apostle Paul was traveling through Asia Minor (Turkey) and Europe. Every culture had its own gods and goddesses, and these religions were mixed together with many expressions of witchcraft and the occult. In many ways, the twenty-first century is very much like the first century. Among many examples of false spiritual pursuits, Paul writes these words to the Colossian Christians:

> See to it that no one takes you captive by philosophy and empty deceit, according to human tradition, according to the elemental spirits of the world, and not according to Christ. (Colossians 2:8)

In what ways might Satan be leading you on the path to spiritual bondage? Are you attracted to instant self-help answers to your problems? Do you follow questionable spiritual leaders who dazzle you or make you feel comfortable with your human desires? Or do you find yourself spending more and more time with God's Word in the Church fellowship?

How do you plan to deal with the reality of false spiritual pursuits in your life? First, with your pastor's guidance, review your exposure to false spiritual teachings in the world and use the Word of Christ as a standard. Remembering Jesus' prediction in Matthew 24 of false prophets deceiving people, apply John's words in his first letter:

Beloved, do not believe every spirit, but test the spirits to see whether they are from God, for many false prophets have gone out into the world. By this you know the Spirit of God: every spirit that confesses that Jesus Christ has come in the flesh is from God, and every spirit that does not confess Jesus is not from God. (1 John 4:1–3)

Second, honestly confess the false spiritual pursuits that have clouded your thinking and led you astray. Claim for yourself God's sure promises to a chastened Israel, confessing their idolatry:

Remember these things, O Jacob, and Israel, for you are My servant; I formed you; you are My servant; O Israel, you will not be forgotten by Me. I have blotted out your transgressions like a cloud and your sins like mist; return to Me, for I have redeemed you. (Isaiah 44:21–23)

Finally, resolve to immerse yourself more regularly in the Word of Christ so that you might love and treasure the true spiritual pursuit of your God, the Father, Son, and Holy Spirit, in a passionate life of praise.

Let the word of Christ dwell in you richly, teaching and admonishing one another in all wisdom, singing psalms and hymns and spiritual songs, with thankfulness in your hearts to God. And whatever you do, in word or deed, do everything in the name of the Lord Jesus, giving thanks to God the Father through Him. (Colossians 3:16–17)

PART THREE

CONFESSING UNGODLY PASSIONS

Blessed is the one whose transgression is
forgiven, whose sin is covered. Blessed is
the man against whom the LORD counts no
iniquity, and in whose spirit there is no deceit.

For when I kept silent, my bones wasted away
through my groaning all day long. For day
and night Your hand was heavy upon me;
my strength was dried up as by the heat of
summer.

I acknowledged my sin to You, and I did not
cover my iniquity; I said, "I will confess my
transgressions to the LORD," and You forgave
the iniquity of my sin. (Psalm 32:1–5)

Part 1 of this book radiated hope and promise through stories
of God working in His people to live with godly passion in the
Word of Christ. Their stories inspired us to seek increased godly
passion in our lives. God's heart beats strongly with our hearts.
This section on the confession of sins prepares our hearts for
understanding God's forgiveness in our beginning and ongoing
study of God's Word.

Part 2 introduced the chilling reality of ungodly passions in the
world and in our sinful selves. Satan orchestrates these passions to
restrain our godly passion and to seek our destruction. This spiritual warfare from outside and from inside came into sharp focus as
we painfully confronted those passions that drain our energy and
those that lead us to bondage. We are drained by time pressures

and high-tech overload; the exhaustion of just surviving, a world out of control, and church letdowns. Materialistic pursuits, sexual and Internet pornography pursuits, sports and leisure pursuits, and false spiritual pursuits all threaten to lead us into bondage. We have a heart problem, which must be fixed. As the psalmist writes, "The troubles of my heart are enlarged" (Psalm 25:17).

In these arenas of spiritual warfare, we learned to see the temptations clearly as Satan's armed assault on our very lives and godly passion. We also placed our confidence in the Word of God to expose our sins, forgive us for Christ's sake, and clothe us with the full armor of God for daily battle.

Now part 3 takes us deeper into Martin Luther's first thesis of his Ninety-five: "The entire life of a believer should be one of repentance." Briefly, we will take stock of ungodly passions in our lives, based on the passions that drain and lead to bondage. Then we will look in depth at David's repentance in Psalm 51 as God restores him for a life of continued joyful service. This section is a guide to discovering and living deeply in the Word of Christ so that we might live with passion for God's will. Psalm 32 quoted above leads us to confess ungodly passions as part of the baptismal life daily and throughout our lives.

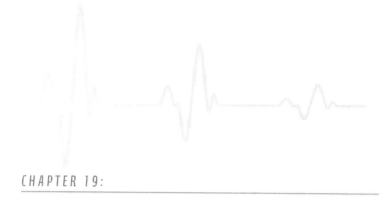

Taking Stock
of Ungodly Passions

> Even if I caused you sorrow by my letter, I
> do not regret it. . . . Yet now I am happy, not
> because you were made sorry, but because your
> sorrow led you to repentance. For you became
> sorrowful as God intended and so were not
> harmed in any way by us. Godly sorrow brings
> repentance that leads to salvation and leaves
> no regret, but worldly sorrow brings death.
> (2 Corinthians 7:8–10 NIV)

In many ways, the second part of this book may have exhausted you. Because you are God's baptized child, the Spirit is working through you every day to thirst for God's Word and seek ways to touch the lives of others. You want to live each moment of every day in faithfulness to God's calling, whether at home, at work, in the Church, or in the community.

The subject of spiritual warfare, though important and realistic, may discourage you in your daily walk. You may have experienced as a hammer blow each area of ungodly passion described in this book—first passions that drain and then passions that lead to bondage. You were led to take stock of your life in each category and offered the rich forgiveness of Christ and promise of Gospel strength for passionate Christ-centered living. Nevertheless, the cumulative effect may leave you wondering about God's love and forgiveness.

Paul encourages the Corinthian Christians in the text quoted above with God's great good news for forgiveness. You see, they had sinned blatantly in many ways, as his first letter describes so graphically. They had permitted an incestuous man to remain as a member in good standing, for example. Paul knew he was causing them pain in his letter because he exposed their sins and urged them to repent and deal with the problem. Then he learned that they had repented, as had the incestuous man. The members of the Church had dealt with and resolved many of their problems. Paul rejoiced in their godly sorrow leading to repentance and salvation. He saw that joyful reality in their restored passion for Christ. They did not pursue worldly sorrow, which only feels bad about personal pain and discomfort but seeks no genuine repentance before God. The easy way becomes the truly sad way. Guilt remains unconfessed. Problems fester and cause infection to set in. The hard way of genuine confession brings forgiveness, peace, and joy with a healed heart.

God uses His Word to help you understand your life in His kingdom, little by little, day by day. As God leads, you repent in small doses of the ungodly passions that drain and lead to bondage. The process of daily repentance refreshes and energizes your daily walk in the forgiveness of Christ. Wearing God's full armor, you can conquer your enemies because God has already defeated them at the cross of Christ.

Recently, I sat in a dental chair for my semiannual teeth cleaning. Never do I enjoy the experience. There have been times when I delayed the experience for multiple years. I told myself that I did not want to spend the money and that I was having no pain at the moment. I took the easy way out, which was not the best way.

On schedule again, I reclined way back in the chair under the intrusive glare of a blinding light. My hygienist began work. She took x-rays to check for cavities. Because of plaque build-up, she used a jet water treatment, which loosened the buildup and made my mouth uncomfortable. Then she began picking and scraping tooth by tooth, inside, outside, lowers, uppers. Blood and debris mixed in my mouth and were suctioned out. Somewhere, as I simply endured the process, I said to her, "You need a great deal of patience to do this, don't you?" She agreed. Before long, she applied a soothing substance as she polished my teeth. The dentist checked my teeth, gave me the okay, and I was free to go. My teeth felt wonderful and clean.

In a flash, I realized that my experience in the dental chair was very much like the daily life of repentance. All too often, I let my unconfessed sin pile up, creating a spiritual cavity with infection and a hardness of heart. I may be on my way to a spiritual root canal and expensive crown, as David describes in Psalm 51. The easy way leads potentially to bondage and death.

When God uses the regular reading of His Word and the counsel of my pastor and other believers, including my dear wife, to help me honestly take stock of ungodly passions and selfish, stubborn attitudes, I find myself in that dental chair under the bright light, confessing my sins. By God's grace for Christ's sake, the ugly buildup is removed patiently by a God who stays by my side to pick and scrape away my sins and apply the soothing salve of forgiveness. In the Divine Service, through His Word and His body and blood, He makes me clean because of the painful, agonizing suffering and death of His Son and the cleansing waters of Baptism in His name.

Yes, I will need to come back to that dental chair again and again for cleansing. Decay continues, but by Christ's blood I am totally clean in the Father's eyes every day, and someday I will stand before Him clean forever. Because of that promise, I can offer a toothy smile each day as He fills me with passion for Christ.

With that Gospel understanding of a life of repentance, we stand ready to go deeply into David's repentance in Psalm 51. He may have something to teach us about passionate living in the Word of Christ.

David's Confession and Ours

David's adultery with Bathsheba and his subsequent murder of her husband, Uriah, provide Scripture's most dramatic evidence of the need for repentance. Because he was king of Israel and a key member of the messianic line leading to Jesus, David's son and David's Lord, David stands at the intersection of human sin and God's saving plan. In 2 Samuel 11:1–27; 12:1–14, we read the sad story of his heinous sin and the compelling account of his confession and forgiveness. In the next two chapters, we look closely at Psalm 51 for David and for us.

THE NEED FOR CLEANSING

Wash me thoroughly from my iniquity, and
cleanse me from my sin! (Psalm 51:2)

Electric dishwashers painlessly produce sparkling plates, once dull and filmy. Electric washing machines with the right detergent turn soiled shirts and blouses into fresh, clean garments. And what of sin? A small problem? A slight stain?

Not so! Think of the sin of David. A king's prerogative to relieve tension? A one-night stand with a beautiful woman? A slight stain of conscience to be washed in the palace laundry? Bathsheba was bathing when he first saw her. "She had been purifying herself from her uncleanness," 2 Samuel 11:4 tells us. Ugly sin protruded. Adultery, the clear charge. Another man's wife was made pregnant by David. The need for cleansing was real. No easy solutions. No human solution. The harder David tried to erase the stain, the more soiled the garment became. Uriah, home on leave at David's command, too much a loyal soldier to cover up David's foul deed. Front-line battle for Uriah, cold-blooded murder. The stain grows and grows. The need for cleansing is now desperate.

What sin stains your heart right now? Less dramatic perhaps than David's adultery and murder. Easier to explain away. Human solutions seem workable. Rationalization. Excuses. The harder you try to erase the stain, the more soiled the garment becomes. Others probably know. Ugly sin protrudes. Certainly you know. And God knows. More than a ritual prayer, you speak with the agonized cry of a terrified sinner, "Wash me thoroughly from my iniquity, and cleanse me from my sin!"

God alone cleanses us from our sin. "The blood of Jesus His Son cleanses us from all sin" (1 John 1:7b). "Though your sins are like scarlet, they shall be as white as snow" (Isaiah 1:18). Since the need for cleansing is so great, thank God for Lent and the Sunday liturgy and the daily reminder of a cleansing Baptism in the name of the Father and of the Son and of the Holy Spirit.

THE TERRIBLE KNOWING

For I know my transgressions, and my sin is
ever before me. (Psalm 51:3)

David knows the depth of his sin—a terrible knowing. He did not start with that knowledge. He knew that all people were sinners. He knew that adultery and murder were sins in the sight of God. He knew that he had committed both sins. However, he does not fully grasp his transgression until the Lord sends Nathan to him with a story about a rich man who takes for himself the only ewe lamb of a poor man. David still doesn't know his transgressions until Nathan says, "You are the man" (2 Samuel 12:7). Now David knows, and he tells Nathan, "I have sinned against the Lord" (2 Samuel 12:13). He acknowledges his sin, a terrible knowing.

Consider the case of a terminally ill woman discovering the nature of her illness, a terrible knowing. She knew that everyone will die sometime. She knew that cancer is often incurable. She knew that she had not been feeling well lately. However, she doesn't know her condition until the doctor announces that she has a terminal illness. Even then, she does not acknowledge her condition until she is able to accept the truth, a terrible knowing.

Jesus says, "I know My own and My own know Me, just as the Father knows Me and I know the Father; and I lay down My life for the sheep" (John 10:14b–15). Paul writes, "That I may know Him and the power of His resurrection" (Philippians 3:10). He adds in his letter to Timothy, "The Lord knows those who are His" (2 Timothy 2:19b). God's terrible knowing of the world's sin is balanced by His Son's complete payment for that sin on our behalf.

THE NAKED CONFESSION

> Against You, You only, have I sinned and done
> what is evil in your sight. (Psalm 51:4a)

Adam and Eve were naked and not ashamed, according to the creation account in Genesis 2. However, soon they were hiding among the trees of the garden and wearing fig leaves. Why the change? They had rebelled against the Lord God by disobeying His command. Adam replies to a questioning God, "I was afraid, because I was naked, and I hid myself" (Genesis 3:10). They cover up not only with fig leaves but also with excuses and passing the blame.

David sinned in his nakedness with Bathsheba, and he started covering up with lies, deception, and murder. His guilt only grew within. Now, confronted by the prophet Nathan, he makes the naked confession, "I have sinned against the LORD" (2 Samuel 12:13). David has sinned against Bathsheba, against Uriah, and against all of Israel. In his confession, David admits his sin against the Lord God. No place to hide. No excuses, no blaming others. God has seen David's naked sin all along, but now David makes a naked confession. Through Nathan, God can say to David, "The LORD also has put away your sin; you shall not die" (verse 13). God accepts David and forgives him. David stands righteous before God because of the Son, the descendant of David, who will someday, stripped of clothing, hang naked on the cross to pay for the world's sin.

Will you make a naked confession of your sin? Fig leaves and trees cannot cover you. Neither will sophistication and makeup. Excuses and blaming others cannot screen God's x-ray vision. We may well have sinned against our spouse or our children or our neighbor or our boss. Ultimately, though, we need to make the naked confession to God. "Against You, You only, have I sinned and done what is evil in Your sight" (Psalm 51:4). God assures us that He has taken away our sins through the Son who died exposed upon the cross. "We are clothed in His righteousness alone, faultless to stand before the throne" (TLH 370:4).

INIQUITY BLOTTED OUT

> Hide Your face from my sins, and blot out all
> my iniquities. (Psalm 51:9)

Oh, the stains that mar our lives—red beet juice on the favorite tie, grease on the white skirt, coffee stains on the linen tablecloth, pet stains on the family room carpet, grass stains on the new tennis shoes, mustard on the car upholstery. Our attempts to blot out those stains often meet with utter frustration. Home remedies, expensive solvents, powerful solutions, and elbow grease take their turn, often making the stain worse. And for every successful stain removal, another stain takes its place.

That's how David must have felt about his sin-stained life. How could he blot out his adultery with Bathsheba and his murder of Uriah? Convicted of his sin by Nathan, David knows he is helpless to remove it. No ritual cleansing will work. Consequently, he cries out to God, "Blot out all my iniquities." Only God can blot out David's sin. God would later say through the prophet Jeremiah, "I will forgive their iniquity, and I will remember their sin no more" (Jeremiah 31:34b). Iniquity is completely blotted out, the stain is removed, the sin is forgotten.

The stain of our sin proves far more troublesome than coffee on a tablecloth. We know the stain exists. Others may not notice, but we see the stains, and so does God: unkind words, selfish actions, ugly thoughts, simmering resentment, green-eyed envy, bitter complaining, and half-hearted worship. All our efforts to blot out these stains only seem to make them more obvious. We cry out to God, "Blot out all my iniquities."

God sent His Son to blot out our iniquities. "He was wounded for our transgressions; He was crushed for our iniquities. . . . The LORD has laid on Him the iniquity of us all" (Isaiah 53:5–6).

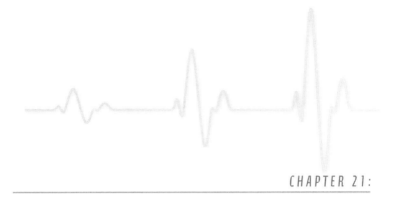

Joy beyond Repentance

David confessed and was assured of forgiveness by God's spokesman, the prophet Nathan. His sin had serious consequences in his family and for the nation, but God's forgiveness was complete. By God's grace, David moved beyond repentance to joyful worship and service as God's anointed king as part of God's saving plan for the world. Notice how Psalm 51 continues.

CREATED AND RENEWED

> Create in me a clean heart, O God, and renew
> a right spirit within me. (Psalm 51:10)

Familiar words, part of the Sunday liturgy, prominent also during Lent. What do these words mean for self-sufficient, stylish, outwardly successful people today? We create jobs, ideas, leisure activities, dream homes, get-rich-quick schemes, and friendships. We make things happen and pull ourselves up by our own bootstraps. Or do we?

David used the word *create* to ask, "Create in me a clean heart, O God." Now on the other side of his tragic affair with Bathsheba, he recognizes his need for cleansing with a terrible knowing that leads to a naked confession. He wants a clean heart to proceed with his life of service as king! He knows the darkness, chaos, and confusion of his heart. He is nothing and can do nothing to make his heart clean. God needs to create in him that clean heart. God alone can make something out of nothing. He alone can bring renewal. "God, who said, 'Let light shine out of darkness,' has shone in our hearts to give the light of the knowledge of the glory of God in the face of Jesus Christ" (2 Corinthians 4:6). The Creator became a creature in the person of Jesus Christ, the second Adam. He lived with a clean heart and willingly died on a cross to bring light out of darkness. With the coming Messiah in view, God created a clean heart in David, granting full forgiveness. David's spirit was renewed for ongoing service as God's king.

"If anyone is in Christ, he is a new creation. The old has passed away; behold, the new has come" (2 Corinthians 5:17). Renouncing our shabby attempts to create our own world, we turn to the Creator who points us to Christ who makes us new. His Spirit restores in us the desire to serve Him and one another.

JOY RESTORED

> Restore to me the joy of Your salvation, and
> uphold me with a willing spirit. (Psalm 51:12)

Instant happiness is the goal of our age. Live life to the fullest. Grab what you want. Enjoy. Make big money. Above all, be happy.

Appealing?

David grabbed for instant happiness, enjoyed a few fleeting moments with another man's wife, and then plunged into a nightmare of guilt, sorrow, and despair. He learned the difference between the fleeting happiness of the moment and God's kind of joy. Repentant, he prays, "Restore to me the joy of Your salvation." Joy has its source outside of David, in God's salvation. God forgives David and preserves his life, even after his dreadful sin. The joy of God's salvation is restored.

What about you? Do you seek that moment of exciting happiness, that forbidden pleasure? Grabbing for the top job at any cost, golf on Sunday mornings, the occasional fling with someone else's spouse, the constant overindulging in food, alcohol, or drugs—fleeting happiness, which can plunge you into a nightmare of guilt, sorrow, and despair?

"Restore to me the joy of Your salvation." A fervent prayer to the God who can turn wailing into dancing and replace sackcloth with the clothing of joy. God's salvation makes the difference—the manger, the Upper Room, the cross, the empty tomb, the font, the altar with bread and wine, the circle of God's people, the reunion before the heavenly throne. Joy overflows from the saving acts of God to produce a peaceful mind, a clean conscience, a voice of praise, ready hands, and a caring smile. He brings lasting joy instead of instant happiness for David and for us.

LIPS OPENED FOR PRAISE

O Lord, open my lips, and my mouth will
declare Your praise. (Psalm 51:15)

Are you having trouble praising God? Do you find yourself going through the motions of worship? Perhaps you blame your lack of musical ability or knowledge of the liturgy. You are in for a surprise. The secret of praise lies with God.

Look at David. He was a master musician, often playing the harp to soothe Saul's fits of rage. He is credited with writing many psalms, a major part of the "hymnbook" of the Church throughout the ages. He obviously was gifted in speech as king and psalm writer. Yet he finds it necessary to ask God to open his lips so he can praise the Lord. Why?

Could it be that David's lips had been sealed from praise because his heart had strayed from God? During the whole Bathsheba incident, he had undoubtedly spoken and perhaps sung many words with his lips but few words of praise to a God who disapproved of his sin. I can imagine David fumbling for words of praise and feeling dry in the mouth and empty in his heart. Having used words of confession to God for his sin, David prays for open lips, and God enables him to praise once again.

Forget about musical ability or a facile tongue. Look to your heart. Confess the wrong kinds of words springing from wrong thoughts and attitudes. Do you find selfishness, indifference, laziness, hardness, impatience, lust, or malice within your heart? With David, pray, "O Lord, open my lips, and my mouth will declare Your praise." He will hear. God sent His Son, Jesus, to begin a new song with His birth, life, death, and resurrection. His cries of loneliness, forgiveness, and completion signal victory over all evil. God places the new song of forgiveness and eternal life in our hearts at Baptism and opens our lips each day to declare His praise in word and song. He accepts our praise because He has accepted Christ's sacrifice for us.

THE SACRIFICE OF BROKENNESS

The sacrifices of God are a broken spirit; a broken and contrite heart, O God, You will not despise. (Psalm 51:17)

Formal sacrifices permeate the pages of the Old Testament, instituted by God with good purpose. However, without the worship of the heart, sacrifices sometimes became mere formalities.

David, a faithful proponent of formal sacrifices, has learned a lesson from his fall into the sins of adultery and murder. He writes, "The sacrifices of God are a broken spirit; a broken and contrite heart, O God, You will not despise." God has broken David's spirit by using the prophet Nathan to convince him of his sin. David has fully confessed his sin before God. In his brokenness, David claims the mercy and promises of God. His broken spirit presents to God a pleasing sacrifice. Now the external sacrifices on the altar reflect the internal spirit of dependence on God for everything.

Are we not sometimes guilty of religious formalism? We think that our external acts—attending church, contributing financial resources, serving on church boards and committees, and so on—count before God as pleasing sacrifices. All the while, we may have haughty, hardened spirits that harbor secret sins and unsavory motives. God knows our hearts and condemns our willful sin. He leads us to brokenness, where we recognize the inadequacy of our sacrifices both internally and externally.

We look to the once-for-all sacrifice of Jesus Christ as the spotless Lamb of God who takes away the sin of the world. God accepts Christ's sacrifice on our behalf. We respond by presenting our bodies as living sacrifices. The external acts remain as a testimony to Christ's sacrifice for us. We worship, give, serve, and love, but we start internally, with the sacrifice of a broken spirit. Broken, we remember the One who was broken for us. We let the sweet savor of His sacrifice permeate our lives to the glory of God.

MOVING ON

David's repentance in Psalm 51 has taught us a great deal about living with godly passion. We want that passion because of God's Spirit within us. Satan seeks to derail and destroy that passion by draining us and leading us to bondage. A life of repentance holds the key to daily and long-term passion for Christ. Only when we live in the Word of Christ can we live a daily baptismal life of repentance. God's heart beats strongly and steadily in our hearts.

From David's experience, we can provide some adjectives to describe godly passion: honest, repentant, humble, forgiven, joyful, and free. We now move on to discover the Word of Christ, live deeply in the Word of Christ, and live God's passion for the world.

PART FOUR

DISCOVERING THE
WORD OF CHRIST

Normally, the word *discovery* suggests finding something new, such as Columbus discovering America or astronauts walking on the moon surface to discover rocks not found elsewhere. Occasionally, *discovery* is used to describe uncovering something long present and searched for but hidden, such as treasure hunters digging up pirate booty or shipwreck entrepreneurs salvaging a sunken vessel.

How does the word *discovery* apply to God's Word, which has been available for centuries in many languages, is the greatest best-seller of all times, and is probably present in your home on a coffee table, at your bedside, or in your study, not to mention electronically on your computer or smartphone? Many today have never been exposed to God's Word at all. They need to discover it. If your Bible lies gathering dust, you need to discover it. If you studied it at one time in your life and think you have read enough, you need to discover it. If you only hear it read and preached at church by someone else, you need to discover it. If you only know bits and pieces of Bible stories and you memorized verses such as John 3:16, you need to discover it.

Don't misunderstand. Whenever God's Word is spoken or read, it is the power of God unto salvation. The Holy Spirit can work through a Bible verse memorized years ago and through Bible stories taught you by your parents or in Sunday School. However, living for Christ in today's culture, which surrounds us with selfish, idolatrous, and manipulative words, requires discovery and rediscovery of hidden treasure, God's Word, which is the Word of Christ. That quest can give you the thrill of adventure as you make discovery after discovery with the Spirit's guidance. As you mature spiritually, your heart will beat more and more in rhythm with God's heartbeat—in other words, with His grace!

First, we learn to live counter culture and to renounce self-help. Then, we hear God's Word calling us, find our passion in His passion, experience God's Word alive in community, and rejoice in the Word of Christ as never before. As a result, we desire to live deeply in the Word of Christ and seek daily to live God's passion for the world.

Living Counter Culture

> Where is the one who is wise? Where is the
> scribe? Where is the debater of this age?
> Has not God made foolish the wisdom
> of the world? For since, in the wisdom of
> God, the world did not know God through
> wisdom, it pleased God through the folly of
> what we preach to save those who believe.
> (1 Corinthians 1:20–21)

Discovering the Word of Christ by the Holy Spirit's power calls for us to live counter culture. The world claims great wisdom and considers the Word of Christ foolish. The apostle Paul recognizes the need to live counter culture—against Jews, who demand miraculous signs before they will believe, and against the Greeks, who demand philosophical wisdom and sophistry, which can be endlessly debated. Paul takes his stand on the Word of Christ:

> We preach Christ crucified, a stumbling block to Jews
> and folly to Gentiles, but to those who are called,
> both Jews and Greeks, Christ the power of God and
> the wisdom of God. (1 Corinthians 1:23–24)

Consider what it means for you to live counter culture. My perspective has been greatly influenced by M. Robert Mulholland

Jr. in his book *Shaped by the Word* (Nashville: The Upper Room, 2001). His concepts helped me evaluate how I have been educated and how I read, which often hinders my reading of Scripture.

"HOW TO READ WITHOUT READING"

All too often, we have been taught to read in such a way that we exercise total control over what we hear and read for our own purposes. On one hand, we read rationally and analytically in judgment of the written or spoken material (as in so-called "objective journalism"). On the other hand, we sometimes read subjectively so that the material is either accepted or rejected based on our personal agenda and needs. When we read God's Word with either controlling approach, we read with our own understanding. Our eyes are blind to see what God is teaching us, and our ears are deaf to hear what He is proclaiming from the Word of Christ.

The prophet Isaiah spoke against a rebellious Israel: " 'Hear, you deaf, and look, you blind, that you may see! . . . He sees many things, but does not observe them; his ears are open, but he does not hear.' The Lord was pleased, for His righteousness' sake, to magnify His law and make it glorious" (Isaiah 42:18, 20–21).

Yet Isaiah's God speaks these words of promise to believers: "I will lead the blind in a way that they do not know, in paths that they have not known I will guide them. I will turn the darkness before into light, the rough places into level ground. These are the things I do, and I do not forsake them" (Isaiah 42:16). God wants to shape us by His Word so that our eyes are opened and our ears unstopped. He helps us to give up our control over His Word and listen to Him speaking to our heart and spirit. What a discovery! How refreshing to receive the Word of Christ!

UNLEARNING BAD READING HABITS

When I learned to master reading, I was challenged to cover as much as possible as quickly as possible: in other words, speed reading. I remember sitting in a reading laboratory at a machine, with light moving through a printed page and which could be set at different speeds, to increase my speed and testing comprehension. There is value in being able to scan material to determine its worth. No doubt that ability helped me deal with college courses that required extensive reading. Today, with the overload of information in print and on the Internet, speed reading helps us discriminate quickly to avoid being deluged with worthless words. However, when applied to reading the Scriptures, speed reading can simply provide another way to stand in judgment of what God's Spirit might be wanting to teach us. In one sense, my cognitive knowledge of God's Word may have been extensive through all of my seminary courses, which used the original languages of Hebrew and Greek as well as survey courses of Old and New Testaments. However, that knowledge, often gained by speed reading, sometimes immunized me against having an open heart to receive God's message for me.

When I learned to read the Scriptures on a regular basis in smaller segments, holding single sentences or phrases in my mind and heart, I discovered more and more the hidden treasures of God's love for me in Christ with its application to my daily life. For more than forty years, I have been reading five psalms and one chapter of Proverbs per day. God has taught me so much over a lifetime of experiences from His Word, a few verses a day—the opposite of speed reading.

Second, I was taught to read analytically and critically, standing in judgment over whatever text I was studying. I wanted to master that text. Whether the subject was history, English literature, science, sociology, or political science, I attempted to establish the historical context and range of scholarly interpretations of the text so I could arrive at a balanced understanding, which I would then accept, reject, or modify as I chose. As with speed reading, this reasoned approach has merit for liberal arts investigation. God has given us minds as part of His creation, and He wants us to use them in His service.

However, when we seek to master the texts of Holy Scripture by using a judgmental approach, in which we decide what to accept or reject or modify for our own purposes, we elevate our human reason over God's revelation, quench the Spirit from using the text to shape our minds and heart, and ultimately fail to see God's Word as the Word of Christ for our salvation.

Paul writes so clearly to the Corinthian Christians about God-given wisdom:

> Yet among the mature we do impart wisdom, although it is not a wisdom of this age or of the rulers of this age, who are doomed to pass away. But we impart a secret and hidden wisdom of God, which God decreed before the ages for our glory. None of the rulers of this age understood this, for if they had, they would not have crucified the Lord of glory. But, as it is written, "What no eye has seen, nor ear heard, nor the heart of man imagined, what God has prepared for those who love Him"—these things God has revealed to us through the Spirit. For the Spirit searches everything, even the depths of God. (1 Corinthians 2:6–10)

We humbly place all of our rational powers of analysis and understanding as well as our open hearts in the care of God's Spirit. He then gives us wisdom to understand God's wonderful saving plan through His Son, Jesus, in the texts of God's Word. We are shaped by His Word to serve Him with our minds and hearts in a foolish world needing rescue.

I thank God for Dr. Martin Franzmann, who taught me in a graduate course called "The Posture of the Interpreter." Dr. Franzmann, by God's grace, had studied Holy Scripture for a lifetime in the original languages, and he expected us to know and use all biblical tools available for the course. Yet the heart of the course focused on treasuring the texts as God's absolutely reliable inspired Word and assuming a posture of humility, placing all scholarly study in the service of God's Spirit revealing Christ in the Word. What a discovery! How refreshing to receive the Word of Christ!

A COUNTER-CULTURE STORY
DR. CHARLES HOHENBERG

My name is Charles Hohenberg. I am a scientist, and I believe in the Word of Christ. My journey began in Selma, Alabama: my birthplace. Enrolled in public schools until my eleventh grade, I transferred to Indian Springs School, near Birmingham. I attended Princeton University, graduating in 1962, and went on to graduate school at the University of California, Berkeley, obtaining my PhD in Physics in 1968. I remained in Berkeley as a post-doctoral scientist for two more years, making sampling equipment and preparations for the first Apollo mission to the moon. Living in Berkeley during those turbulent times of the '60s provided an initiation of sorts to the cross-currents experienced by a scientist who follows Christ. From Berkeley, I joined the faculty at Washington University in St. Louis, where I remain a professor of physics and active in my research until today, some forty-one years later. Continuously funded by NASA, my research has centered on the formation and evolution of the early solar system, leading me to become part of the science teams of both the Genesis and the Stardust NASA missions. My research has resulted in about three hundred scientific publications and the supervision of thirteen graduate students who obtained their PhD degrees under my guidance. Four of them now have tenured faculty positions at major universities, three went on to work in the Los Alamos and Lawrence Livermore National Labs, and one became group leader for nuclear safeguards that secure and monitor plutonium from the disassembled nuclear weapons of the arsenal of the former Soviet Union. My journey with Christ was shaped by all of these things but really began at an early age.

While growing up in Alabama, I attended Sunday School and church with my family. I remember the felt boards with Noah and the animals. I remember the feeling of being reenergized for doing my homework after church, and I discovered the power of prayer. Both of these seemed to be God's messages to me at that early age, letting me know that "I am there" and extending an invitation to a growing relationship with Him. Whatever was His plan, exposure to God's Word through church and my family set the stage for a life in which my journey with God continued to grow. As a sinner, I continued to stumble, but God was there. While growing up, I felt my life blessed by His undeserved love and forgiving grace, but I continued to be headstrong and proud. After working on a particularly hard project with good results or upon receiving federal support from a grant proposal I had written, I would go to church with anticipation, only to find emptiness there. Then, later, I would realize that the pride I felt was self-directed, not God-directed. We can never measure up, and when we think we do, He shows us our weakness: It is not the accomplishments we make and our pride in doing so that save us; it is the gift of God through Christ that takes a failed human and gives him or her love and encouragement. This should bring humility on us, not pride. I have learned to listen more to His Word, not to what I want it to say, or even to imagine that I fully understand what it says, because it provides fresh new knowledge with each reading—truly a living Word. When two or more Christians gather, God is there: a blessing that is all the more evident in the LifeLight study group. With the LifeLight family of Christians, the Word comes alive, as it always does, with fresh new insights amplified by Dr. Carter and the group. In LifeLight, God speaks not only the power of Christ's sacrifice on the cross and the depth of His love, but He also speaks into the hearts of each of us individually.

However, being a scientist and a Christian brings me face-to-face with the question of how science can be compatible with God. If we, as scientists, can explain the workings of the universe, why do we need God? Indeed, almost all scientists I have known not only are atheists but also look down their noses at scientists who are Christian.

A scientist investigates the universe and describes it in mathematical terms. Therefore, what need does he or she have for God? This seems to be the position of many scientists. I look at God and science from the other perspective, and I question how it can be that good scientists aren't all Christian. All it takes is a warm summer night when I can lie down on a blanket and look up at the heavens, and I am reminded that this is what David must have done, marveling at the handiwork of the Creator, whom we might be able to describe but can never explain.

Many scientists marvel at how much progress they have made in understanding the laws of physics and chemistry. They can describe many things by those laws. Appreciating a beautiful house does not put you on par with the architect who designed it. To me, the laws of physics express the beauty and intricacies of God's creation. How can scientists avoid belief in God when they see His work all around them? He shows them new wonders that should humble them, not elevate their pride in their new knowledge (and to believe there is no need for God to explain these things).

In the scientific community, being a believer can be detrimental to your profession. A friend of mine, a department chairman for twenty-six years, once remarked in a job evaluation about a technician responsible for demonstrations in our lectures, "I heard him talking with Jesus." The technician was so good at his job that this made no difference, but the derogatory nature of the comment is evident. I have given lectures to the (relatively small, but growing) group of Christian graduate students about science and religion. I was looking for some papers by a scientist at Los Alamos National Lab, a good friend of mine and the co-principal investigator of the Genesis space mission. I found on the Internet a long, carefully written paper about Christianity and science, about why scientists should all be Christian. I have since discussed that paper with several others here at Washington University. Christians are indeed quietly making their presence known in science, but it is a long road to travel and there is much arrogance and hostility along the way. Only the living Word provides the courage to find other Christians in science with the courage to feed Christ's sheep while ignoring persecution by their colleagues and others. This Word is painted afresh as we traveled through 1 Peter in our LifeLight group. That Word of Christ provides God-given encouragement. The light of the Lord shining from a fellow scientist can illuminate the path of truth: that the heavens above me display the wonders of the Lord, not the understanding of man. While a visitor to a museum may describe a beautiful work of art, it is the artist that is the creator; the visitor is an admirer. In science, man must be considered the tourist and God the creator.

Renouncing Self-Help

> The hand of the LORD was upon me, and He
> brought me out in the Spirit of the LORD and
> set me down in the middle of the valley; it was
> full of bones. And He led me around among
> them, and behold, there were very many on
> the surface of the valley, and behold, they were
> very dry. And He said to me, "Son of man, can
> these bones live?" And I answered, "O Lord
> GOD, You know." (Ezekiel 37:1–3)

Our culture deifies a self-help approach to life. Bookstore shelves
are filled with books on pop psychology, releasing the power of
your mind, practical guidelines for success in dating, marriage,
social relationships, job-hunting, corporate promotions, dieting,
building strong and beautiful bodies, and gourmet cooking. Do-
it-yourself carpentry, plumbing, and interior decorating books
add to the list. Cable and public television channels provide self-
help tips, as do numerous Web sites. There is nothing wrong
in itself with these practical guidelines. However, when a self-
help approach claims religious significance and promises all
you need for life and death apart from the true God, it becomes
idolatry. Unfortunately, many Christian books, intending to give
guidance for Christian living, create the false impression that

we can spiritually pull ourselves up by our own bootstraps. Yet the essence of living with passion in the Word of Christ involves renouncing self-help.

You see, Ezekiel's God-given vision of the valley of dry bones describes a nation as bones scattered in a valley, very dry and hopelessly dead. God interprets this vision for Ezekiel as applying to the rebellious house of Israel. They have tried every self-help remedy available—relying on their own wisdom, seeking political alliances with other nations, and engaging in a variety of idolatrous practices. Now the Southern Kingdom of Judah has been conquered by the Babylonians, their temple and city walls are destroyed, and the remaining people are taken as captives to exile in Babylon. God says, "Son of man, these bones are the whole house of Israel. Behold, they say, 'Our bones are dried up, and our hope is lost; we are indeed cut off' " (Ezekiel 37:11).

UNLEARNING ANOTHER
BAD READING HABIT

Because of our cultural upbringing, we often come to Scripture with a problem-solving mentality. Accustomed to cookbooks, practical business guidelines, and even online medical recommendations for self-care, we look at the Bible as a guidebook or set of rules for godly living. We expect from the Bible immediate answers to solve our current problems. Either we grasp at straws and find solutions that support what we already think we should do, or we walk away disillusioned because the answers don't seem to jump out at us. We might even chastise God for not solving our problems in our way of thinking.

Isaiah describes this approach very candidly:

> For they are a rebellious people, lying children, children unwilling to hear the instruction of the

> LORD; who say to the seers, "Do not see," and to the
> prophets, "Do not prophesy to us what is right; speak
> to us smooth things, prophesy illusions, leave the
> way, turn aside from the path, let us hear no more
> about the Holy One of Israel!" (Isaiah 30:9–11)

Scripture brings us focus on God, not on solutions to our problems. Often, God first shows us our rebellion against Him as we rely on self-help. That leads us to our place in the valley of dry bones. Then, He can open our eyes to the mystery of His undeserved love for us, delivered with unbelievable power.

"Prophesy over these bones, and say to them, 'O dry bones, hear the word of the LORD.' " (Ezekiel 37:4. Then a rattling sound was heard as the dry bones came together and took on tendons and flesh, followed by breath from the four winds to bring life to the slain. God then gives this incredible promise of deliverance:

> Behold, I will open your graves and raise you from
> your graves, O My people. And I will bring you into
> the land of Israel. And you shall know that I am the
> LORD, when I open your graves, and raise you from
> your graves, O My people. And I will put My Spirit
> within you, and you shall live, and I will place you in
> your own land. Then you shall know that I am the
> LORD; I have spoken, and I will do it, declares the
> LORD. (Ezekiel 37:12–14)

God provided Himself to His people in their desperate need by bringing them home to live for Him in many practical ways. His Word opened to them the mystery of His promised salvation through a coming Messiah, and with that promise came all they needed for daily life in His service—worship, rebuilding the temple and city walls, rereading the Old Testament Scripture, bearing witness to the nations, and waiting patiently for the Messiah.

When we lay our problems and needs before our Father, renouncing self-help as the solution, He assures us that we have been brought from death to life through Jesus' death and resurrection. Then the Spirit opens His Word to us so we learn more and more about the mystery of His love. In the process, the Word of Christ supplies all we need for daily life in His service: practical, life-giving help from Him to face each day's problems in His grace. What a discovery! How refreshing to receive the Word of Christ!

"BREAKING THE CRUST"

The last two chapters have brought us face-to-face with a critical personal problem that threatens our ongoing discovery of the Word of Christ. The surrounding culture teaches us pagan ways of dealing with truth and wisdom apart from God; hence the need to live counter culture. We develop a hard, outer crust, formed around us by the world's manipulative mindset; hence the need to renounce self-help as we approach God's Word. Only God can break through that crust of self through His powerful Word to bring us life and salvation. The writer to the Hebrews helps end this chapter with promised rest and the assurance that God will break our crust of self to open for us the Word of Christ:

> So then, there remains a Sabbath rest for the people of God, for whoever has entered God's rest has also rested from his works as God did from His. Let us therefore strive to enter that rest, so that no one may fall by the same sort of disobedience. For the word of God is living and active, sharper than any two-edged sword, piercing to the division of soul and of spirit, of joints and marrow, and discerning the thoughts

HEARTBEAT!: Living with Passion in the Word of Christ

and intentions of the heart. And no creature is
hidden from His sight, but all are naked and exposed
to the eyes of Him to whom we must give account.
(Hebrews 4:9–13)

Hearing God's Word Calling Us

Now the young man Samuel was ministering to the LORD under Eli. And the word of the LORD was rare in those days. . . . Now Samuel did not yet know the LORD, and the word of the LORD had not yet been revealed to him. . . . And the LORD came and stood, calling as at other times, "Samuel! Samuel!" And Samuel said, "Speak, for Your servant hears." (1 Samuel 3:1, 7, 10)

This chapter explores how God has spoken to you in your life through the Word of Christ. I was brought by my Christian parents to the waters of Baptism, where the pastor's words "I baptize you in the name of the Father and of the Son and of the Holy Spirit" brought me into His kingdom through water and the Word. That Word of Christ was imprinted on my heart in many ways as I grew up—Bible stories I learned at home, at church, and in a Christian school; Bible verses I memorized and recited; songs and hymns I sang in school and church, including participating in an annual children's Christmas Eve service. God's Word was calling me to listen and learn as His child through Baptism. He began to shape my life by His Word.

That is how the Lord spoke to the young boy Samuel and set him apart for a life of service as a prophet in Israel. The Word of the Lord was rare because Israel and its leaders such as Eli had turned away from the Lord. By God's grace, Samuel heard the Word of the Lord and responded with a life of obedience.

Spend some time reflecting on how God has been calling you in your life through His Word. The hymnwriter Jaroslav Vajda helps us reflect on how God uses Christmas to bring us the saving message of Christ:

Son of God, which Christmas is it
that we share this year?
Will it grow with new reflections,
Will it bring You near?
Will I marvel; What a favor!
What a gift, Only God can give!

Jesus, bless the ones who told me
how You came to earth,
Why You left Your heavenly dwelling
For a human birth.
Do I marvel; What a favor!
What a gift! Only God can give!

Jesus, bless the ones who taught me
all the songs I sing:
of the angels and of Mary,
and the infant king,
Do I marvel! What a favor!
What a gift only God can give!

Jesus, bless the ones who hurry
from the stable light

with the story of Your glory,
brightening the night.
Share the marvel: Love's best favor!
Love's best gift anyone can give!

(Jaroslav Vajda, "Son of God, Which Christmas Is It?")

With these simple but powerful words, Vajda helps us discover how God's Word has been calling us over the years through people who have taught us the Christmas story and Christmas songs and how we can pass God's Word on to others, including children and grandchildren. The Word of Christ calls us again and again throughout our lives. What a discovery! How refreshing to receive the Word of Christ!

To help you reflect on your discoveries of God's Word in your life, hear the following stories of how individual Bible verses have touched individual lives and enabled them to use these verses for witness to others.

MARK AND PSALM 37:5

Commit thy way unto the LORD; trust also in Him;
and He shall bring it to pass. (Psalm 37:5 KJV)

When my son, Mark, was thirteen years old, we traveled to Indianapolis to spend some quality time together as father and son at a time when my mother was hospitalized with cancer. While there, my mother died from a sudden stroke. At the funeral, Pastor Maas used Mom's confirmation verse as his text: "Commit thy way unto the LORD; trust also in Him; and He shall bring it to pass." During the service, Mark asked me if he could have that verse as his confirmation text. Obviously his grandma's faith in Jesus and lifelong walk with the Lord had moved him to make that request. As Mark's pastor in Peru, Indiana, I was able to grant his request at his confirmation several months later.

Twelve years later to the day of Mom's funeral, Mark was married in Rochester, Minnesota. In a brief message as his father, I quoted that favorite Bible passage, Psalm 37:5, as guidance for the newlyweds. Tears formed in Mark's eyes as he remembered. A few days ago my only brother, Stan, died in Indianapolis. Mark drove there for the funeral, joining his sister, Amy, in support of us. At the family burial plot, both of us looked at the grave of my mother and saw those familiar words, "Commit thy way unto the LORD," engraved on her stone. God's Spirit had given faith in Jesus Christ as Savior to Mom, Mark, and me as His baptized children. Flowing from that trust comes a commitment to walk in His ways and witness His love to our family and friends.

In Psalm 37, David, attacked by foes and aware of his own sins, looks back over his life and sees the Lord as his stronghold and his hope for the future. Gladly he commits his way to the Lord and trusts His saving promises.

BECKY AND JEREMIAH 29:11

"For I know the plans I have for you," declares the LORD, "plans to prosper you and not to harm you, plans to give you hope and a future." (Jeremiah 29:11 NIV)

This Bible verse requires two devotions because of its powerful impact on our family and many others. Our youngest daughter, Becky, was diagnosed with aplastic anemia in 1989 and died three and a half years later at twenty-three years of age. In early 1992, as she was preparing to graduate from college, she was receiving more frequent blood transfusions.

On a March Monday I received a letter of encouragement from a fellow pastor in New York. It included a bookmark containing the words of Jeremiah 29:11. When I called Becky that day to hear the latest news on her blood counts, I decided to share the passage with her. She said, "I also have a verse to share with you. You go first." I shared Jeremiah 29:11 with her, and there was dead silence on the phone line. She simply said, 'That's my verse too.' The very same day she had received the same verse in the mail from her former high school journalism teacher. From that point on, Jeremiah 29:11 became our favorite Bible verse: " 'For I know the plans I have for you,' declares the LORD, 'plans to prosper you and not to harm you, plans to give you hope and a future.' " We were praying that Becky's future would include healing from her aplastic anemia, but we knew that God loved her deeply and had won salvation for her through the death and resurrection of Jesus Christ.

Becky shared that verse with other students in a Bible study and wrote about it in the newspaper of her former high school. We got extra copies of the bookmark to remind us and share with others. In a Seattle hospital, we had occasion to use Jeremiah 29:11 in conversation with other family members whose loved ones were receiving bone marrow transplants—always pointing to Jesus as our Savior.

JEREMIAH 29:11 LIVES ON

"For I know the plans I have for you," declares the LORD, "plans to prosper you and not to harm you, plans to give you hope and a future." (Jeremiah 29:11 NIV)

Our daughter Becky died on January 9, 1993, from bone marrow transplant complications, but our favorite Bible verse, Jeremiah 29:11, lives on. At the funeral, the pastor used it as a text. Becky's fiancé and her former high school math teacher independently referred to it also. Invited to lead chapel at Concordia Lutheran High School, Fort Wayne, which had supported Becky with prayer and cards, I was asked to use Jeremiah 29:11 as a text. That spring, the Concordia girls' track team sent us their special T-shirts with Jeremiah 29:11 on the back. We have as gifts in our home a framed picture with Jeremiah 29:11 in calligraphy and a folio page from the 1640 King James Version of that chapter. The gravestone with Becky's name and ours features Jeremiah 29:11.

When I was asked to speak about and teach Bible studies on Jeremiah 29:11, I studied the passage carefully in its context. The remnant of Judah, feeling hopeless in Babylonian exile because of the repeated sins of idolatry in their homeland, receives a letter from Jeremiah, urging them to prepare for a long stay in exile, remaining faithful in prayer and worship of the God of Israel. Then, to these repentant believers, Jeremiah delivers the Lord's message of plans to give His people "hope and a future," in the short term, a return to Israel after seventy years, and in the long term, from the very heart of God, eternal salvation through the death and resurrection of Jesus, the promised Messiah.

Yes, Jeremiah 29:11 lifted up Becky and our family in critical times and continues to touch lives with the Good News of Jesus Christ. We call that verse the gift that keeps on giving.

STAN AND REVELATION 3:11

Hold fast what you have, so that no one may seize your crown. (Revelation 3:11b)

My brother, Stan, died on April 10, 2011, at age 62 after a long struggle of eleven years, which was begun by a major disabling stroke. During that time, he served productively in many ways, reached out to countless people where he lived, including his home near a small town, assisted living facilities, and nursing homes, and faithfully went to worship among God's people. As the end approached, his daughter asked about any Bible texts or hymns he would choose for his funeral. Without hesitation, he selected Revelation 3:11, which the pastor then used at his funeral: "I am coming soon. Hold fast what you have, so that no one may seize your crown."

In John's Book of Revelation, these words are addressed to the Church in Philadelphia. Although the Christians there have little strength, God promises to be with them in the hour of trial and give them the crown of life through faith in Jesus when He comes again. He urges them to remain faithful in difficult times.

I believe Stan wanted that Bible verse not only as a testimony to God's saving grace in his own life's struggles, but also, more importantly, as a message to his daughters and other family members and friends to "hold fast what you have, so that no one may seize your crown." Responsive to Stan's witness, his two-and-half-year-old granddaughter was baptized in his room the day before he died, and the clear message of salvation was proclaimed at his funeral. Revelation 3:11—a favorite Bible verse for my brother, Stan, and a witness to many!

What is your favorite Bible verse? How did it become meaningful to you? Have you ever thought of this verse as a tool for witness of your faith in Jesus Christ as Savior?

Perhaps an important first step in discovering the Word of Christ is joining young Samuel each day with the expectant words, "Speak, Lord, for Your servant hears!" (see 2 Samuel 3:10). He continues calling us through His Word to renounce self-help and live counter culture as we walk on paths untrod. The psalmist writes, "Your testimonies are my heritage forever, for they are the joy of my heart" (Psalm 119:111).

Finding Our Passion in His Passion

> You search the Scriptures because you think
> that in them you have eternal life; and it is
> they that bear witness about Me, yet you refuse
> to come to Me that you may have life. (John
> 5:39–40)

Discovering God's Word in all its truth and purity always means discovering it as the Word of Christ. From Genesis in the Old Testament to Revelation in the New Testament, God's Word is the Word of Christ. After healing a man at the Pool of Bethesda on the Sabbath, Jesus came under intense condemnation from the Jewish leaders because they believed He had violated the Law of Moses. Jesus then denounced them for not seeing God's Word as the Word of Christ. He accused them in their diligent study of the Scriptures word by word and letter by letter. Yet, says Jesus, "it is they that bear witness about Me" (John 5:39).

How do you approach God's Word—as an important literary document to study, as an ancient book of history, as a code of moral laws to be obeyed, as a guidebook for practical living, or as the Word of Christ? The eyewitnesses of Jesus' death and resurrection clearly see Him as the fulfillment of the Old Testament Scriptures and boldly proclaim Jesus as the only way to salvation. In his Pentecost sermon, Peter quotes frequently from the Hebrew

Scriptures (Joel, Isaiah, and Psalms) to reach the following con-clusion, which brought many to repentance: "Let all the house of Israel therefore know for certain that God has made Him both Lord and Christ, this Jesus whom you crucified" (Acts 2:36). To their repentant cry, he asserts, "Repent and be baptized every one of you in the name of Jesus Christ for the forgiveness of your sins, and you will receive the gift of the Holy Spirit. For the promise is for you and for your children and for all who are far off, everyone whom the Lord our God calls to Himself" (Acts 2:38–39). For Peter, God's Word is the Word of Christ.

John makes a similar confession about God's Word: "That which was from the beginning, which we have heard, which we have seen with our eyes, which we looked upon and have touched with our hands, concerning the word of life. . . . And the blood of Jesus His Son cleanses us from all sin" (1 John 1:1, 7b).

The apostle Paul, who as a former Pharisee was well-versed in the Old Testament Scriptures, says to the Corinthians, "For I decided to know nothing among you except Jesus Christ and Him crucified" (1 Corinthians 2:2). God's Word is the Word of Christ, which means forgiveness of sins, life, and salvation.

For that reason, when we seek godly passion for our lives both now and in the long term, we can only find our passion in His pas-sion. The more we read and study God's Word in Old and New Testaments, the more we see it as the Word of Christ, God's plan from before creation unfolding little by little and building toward a climax. Waiting believers discover Jesus of Nazareth as the Word made flesh, the Son of Man, the promised Messiah, the Suffering Servant, and the risen and ascended Lord.

In many ways, our passion grows when we let God's Spirit enfold our story in His story. Growing up, I found great meaning in the rhythms of the Church Year: Advent, Christmas, Epiphany, Lent, Holy Week, Easter, and Pentecost. I learned Bible stories at my mother's knee. My parents brought me to church every Sunday where I learned to sing and memorize the liturgy. They placed me in a Christian school where I learned Scripture verses and Luther's Catechism. I also participated in children's Christmas services and youth choirs. Always Christ's death and resurrection was the heart of my spiritual life. Year after year, I became part of God's salvation story. One of the most powerful memories of my youth was participating in an annual Easter pageant at the Fairground Coliseum in Indianapolis, started by my pastor. I first participated by singing in a mass children's choir, then donning a costume as part of the multitude waving palm branches while Jesus entered on a real donkey. Before going off to college, I also was a Pharisee and finally one of Jesus' disciples, James the Less. Each role drew me deeper and deeper into Christ's Passion for my salvation by God's grace for Christ's sake through faith. So transformed was I by the Easter pageant that as a pastor in Peru, Indiana, years later, I started a similar Easter pageant in the local high school auditorium, which was still going twenty-five years later. My children were able to experience Jesus' Passion also.

Just last year, Gail and I led a tour group to the Passion Play in Oberammergau, a small village in southern Germany near Munich. Delivered from the Black Plague in 1633, villagers made a vow to present a day-long passion play every ten years in thanksgiving to God. Their continued dedication to the Passion Play, a monumental effort, bears witness to the Word of Christ. We spent two nights in Oberammergau, meeting villagers who take on roles in the play and host visitors from around the world. My passion to live for Christ once again increased because of this remembrance of Christ's Passion on my behalf.

This year, our LifeLight community spent eighteen weeks studying the sixty-six chapters of Isaiah, concluding with a study of 1 and 2 Peter. I close this chapter with quotes from Isaiah 53 and 1 Peter 2. Can there be any doubt that Christ's Passion is central to Scripture or that God's Word is always the Word of Christ?

He was despised and rejected by men; a man of sorrows, and acquainted with grief; and as one from whom men hide their faces He was despised, and we esteemed Him not.

Surely He has borne our griefs and carried our sorrows; yet we esteemed Him stricken, smitten by God, and afflicted. But He was wounded for our transgressions; He was crushed for our iniquities; upon Him was the chastisement that brought us peace, and with His stripes we are healed. All we like sheep have gone astray; we have turned—every one—to his own way; and the LORD has laid on Him the iniquity of us all.

He was oppressed, and He was afflicted, yet He opened not His mouth; like a lamb that is led to the slaughter, and like a sheep that before its shearers is silent, so He opened not His mouth. (Isaiah 53:3–7)

For to this you have been called, because Christ also suffered for you, leaving you an example, so that you might follow in His steps. He committed no sin, neither was deceit found in His mouth. When He was reviled, He did not revile in return; when He suffered, He did not threaten, but continued entrusting Himself to Him who judges justly. He Himself bore our sins in His body on the tree, that we might die to sin and live to righteousness. By His wounds you have been healed. For you were straying like sheep, but have now returned to the Shepherd and Overseer of your souls. (1 Peter 2:21–25)

Christ's saving Passion on the cross for us flows from His compassion, as Matthew writes, "When He saw the crowds, He had compassion for them, because they were harassed and helpless, like sheep without a shepherd" (Matthew 9:36). The writer to the Hebrews adds, "We do not have a high priest who is unable to sympathize with our weaknesses, but one who in every respect has been tempted as we are, yet was without sin" (Hebrews 4:15).

The sinless Savior sympathizes with us because He was tempted like we are, and He shows compassion on straying sheep. Therefore, God gives us another adjective to describe living with passion, following Christ's example of suffering on our behalf—compassionate. Our story is wrapped up in His story! We find our passion in His passion! His heart beats in our hearts!

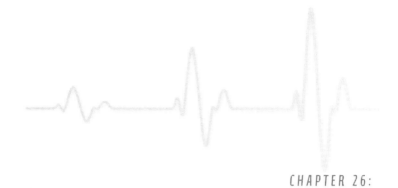

Experiencing God's Word Alive in Community

> Let the word of Christ dwell in you richly, teaching and admonishing one another in all wisdom, singing psalms and hymns and spiritual songs, with thankfulness in your hearts to God. (Colossians 3:16)

God's Word may indeed call us in the privacy of our home or office, even as He called Samuel, Isaiah, and Jeremiah. God uses Bible reading and prayer in our daily devotional life to strengthen our faith in Christ as Savior. We especially experience God's Word alive in community, the fellowship of believers—worship, biblical preaching and teaching, group Bible study, and the honest, caring interactions of Christian fellowship in a variety of settings. Paul writes to the Colossian Christians:

> We always thank God, the Father of our Lord Jesus Christ, when we pray for you, since we heard of your faith in Christ Jesus and of the love that you have for all the saints, because of the hope laid up for you in heaven. Of this you have heard before in the word of the truth, the gospel, which has come to you, as indeed in the whole world it is bearing fruit and growing—as it also does among you, since the

day you heard it and understood the grace of God in truth. (Colossians 1:3–6)

What a testimony to God's Word alive in community! Paul clearly proclaims the crucified and risen Christ as the heart of the Gospel, received through Baptism. He continues in his letter to apply that Gospel to every aspect of practical daily life, and then he challenges the Christian community, "Let the word of Christ dwell in you richly, teaching and admonishing one another in all wisdom" (Colossians 3:16).

In what ways have you experienced God's Word alive in community? Think of specific and concrete examples from your experiences growing up in family and religious instruction, from more recent worship and Bible study, and from conversations with Christian friends in times of joy or grief, accomplishments or struggles. How has God's Spirit made the Word of Christ dwell in you richly?

This chapter provides some stories of God's Word alive in community to aid your reflection. Recently, I asked members of our Wednesday men's group why they came to study books such as Isaiah and 1 and 2 Peter week after week and year after year. One replied, "I get so much more out of Bible study in a group. I read the Bible at home and sometimes struggle to understand certain sections of Scripture. But when a book of the Bible is taught in this group, I learn a great deal from the questions and comments of the rest of you. Your experience and faith shine through and help me articulate my own questions and application to life."

Others in the Tuesday evening couples' group have observed, "I never studied the Bible before at all, and I have so many questions. Now I am able to share my study with others and learn from their answers. Prayer together is so important. The honesty of the group helps me look at my own life and my need for Christ. I see God working in their lives and am encouraged to trust Him for the problems and challenges in my life. I understand God's Word better now than I did, though I still have so much to learn. And I now see Christ throughout Scripture as my Savior."

IN THE CATACOMBS

> But you are a chosen race . . . that you may proclaim the excellencies of Him who called you out of darkness into His marvelous light. (1 Peter 2:9)

On a recent trip to Italy, we visited the Catacombs of St. Sebastian, just outside the walls of ancient Rome. Our tour led us deep into the darkness and the narrow passages of the catacombs, where many early Christians lie buried, some individually and some in family groupings. At one location, we were told that Christians gathered there for worship. There on the wall, we saw rough drawings of Jesus and His disciples celebrating the Last Supper and stick figures of sheep and the Good Shepherd.

As we emerged into the light, my heart was stirred by the silent witness of that early community of believers, persecuted for their faith, forced to bury their dead outside the city walls, but by their words and actions "[proclaiming] the excellencies of Him who called [them] out of darkness into His marvelous light." In their Baptism, they were connected with the "living stone rejected by men but in the sight of God chosen and precious" (1 Peter 2:4), formed as "a chosen race, a royal priesthood, a holy nation, a people for His own possession" (verse 9). "As sojourners and exiles" (verse 11), they were enabled by God's grace, fortified at the Lord's Table, to "keep [their] conduct among the Gentiles honorable" (verse 12), so that their enemies might "see [their] good deeds and glorify God on the day of visitation" (verse 12).

In today's twenty-first-century world, with its pagan beliefs and lifestyle, we have the privilege of "[proclaiming] the excellencies of Him who called you out of darkness into His marvelous light." As aliens and strangers in the world, sometimes persecuted, often rejected, we are, by virtue of our Baptism into Jesus' death and resurrection, a chosen people belonging to God.

WHERE GENERATIONS MEET

But as for me and my house, we will serve the LORD. (Joshua 24:15c)

How is God's Word alive across the generations in your family? Perhaps you might begin by reflecting on events or locations where the generations meet.

On several occasions, Gail and I have met our children and grandchildren at a pizza buffet: abundant food, fun, and a place to relate. Busch Stadium, home of the St. Louis Cardinals, comes to mind. I took Mark, Amy, and Becky there when they were young. Now we repeat the experience with our grandchildren. There is much anticipation, conversation with nachos during the game, and memories afterward. A summer vacation together at Silver Dollar City in Branson, Missouri, provided much quality time during the trip, at meals, in the hotel, and at the amusement park. Going to church together in St. Louis, Missouri; Olathe, Kansas; or Minnesota focuses on the importance of Jesus Christ in our lives and witness.

The generations also came together at Shechem in the Promised Land of Canaan. Joshua, near the end of his life, recalls the generations and events of Israel's past: Abraham, Isaac, and Jacob, the Egyptian years, freedom and the wilderness years under Moses and Aaron, the conquest of Jericho, and settling this land of Canaan. Now he addresses the present generation and asks them to choose whom they will serve—idols of the nations or the true God. Joshua's witness across the generations is clear: "But as for me and my house, we will serve the LORD." The people replied, "We also will serve the LORD, for He is our God" (Joshua 24:18).

Whether eating pizza, attending a ball game, vacationing, or worshiping in church, the generational witness is clear: we believe in Jesus as Savior by God's grace. As part of His Holy Church, we worship Him regularly and keep His Word alive in our family, and we will serve Him every day so others may also believe and be saved.

EASTER FAMILY IN JAPAN

> Not neglecting to meet together, as is the habit of some, but encouraging one another, and all the more as you see the Day drawing near. (Hebrews 10:25)

Easter and the family of God. Images from Scripture and Japan. Two weary, disheartened disciples inviting a stranger to their table, only to discover the risen Christ in the breaking of the bread. Their rush to join the Eleven and celebrate the good news (Luke 24:28–35). Strong encouragement from Hebrews to worship regularly (not just on Easter) as the Day of the Lord approaches. Now these words from Bethany Paulus in Japan:

> Easter was a special celebration for me. The service included Easter banners, singing by the choir, and the Baptism of the pastor's granddaughter! Afterward, the church members gathered together for a special lunch and time together. As we ate lunch, I visited with one of the older high school girls. The day before, she had come to the church, and it had been her first time to dye Easter eggs! I usually dye Easter eggs with my family, and she was surprised to hear

that I don't usually dye them with the congregation. But then, she began to explain that she is the only Christian in her family. She told me it would be strange for her to do something like that with her family.

That's when it occurred to me that this church *is* her family. Like many Christians in Japan, she is the only member of her family who is a believer in Jesus. No wonder these believers linger together, celebrating a day and a reason of which many others, including their families, are unaware. They gather to support and encourage one another. This year, Easter has reminded me not only of Christ's death and resurrection but also of the gift of the family of God. My prayer is that God will continue to teach me how to build up and encourage others in His family, especially those in His family here.

GOD'S WORD ALIVE IN COMMUNITY!

These stories of the Christians in the catacombs, families connecting across generations around the Word of Christ, and an Easter family in Japan stimulate us to ponder how God's Word has been, is, and might be alive in community for us, those we love, and those God is leading us to reach for Christ. What a joy to discover the Word of Christ in these settings! God's heartbeat in community!

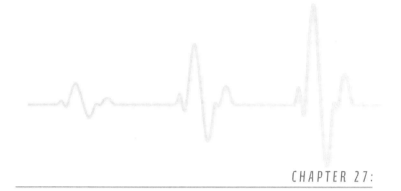

Rejoicing in the Word of Christ

Rejoice in the Lord always; again I will say,
Rejoice. (Philippians 4:4)

This part of the book has described the adventure of discovering the Word of Christ. True adventures present significant obstacles to overcome on the road to a noble end. Indiana Jones takes on the raiders of the lost ark, for example. We have faced Satan's deadly obstacles of the world and our sinful selves. God's Spirit has armed us with the Word of God so that we might live counter culture and renounce self-help in pursuit of "the goal for the prize of the upward call of God in Christ Jesus" (Philippians 3:14). In the process, we have begun hearing God's Word calling us from childhood or as adults to embrace Christ alone for our salvation as His baptized children and to live with passion for Christ. The adventure takes on fresh meaning when we realize that we find our passion only in His passion. His story shapes our story as we are shaped by the Word of God. We then experience God's Word alive in community, where believers share the great adventure of Christ together, surrounded by the Word and prayer.

Finally, God's Spirit moves us to rejoice in the Word of God and again to rejoice. Despite or because of dreadful obstacles, that joy increases in our hearts as we make discovery after discovery in that sure, saving Word. As Paul writes, "Therefore, since we have been justified by faith, we have peace with God through our Lord Jesus Christ. Through Him we have also obtained access by faith into this grace in which we stand, and we rejoice in hope of the glory of God" (Romans 5:1–2). Expect to find increasing joy in your adventure in the Word of God.

AN EVERY-SUNDAY GLAD

> I was glad when they said to me,
> "Let us go to the house of the LORD!"
> (Psalm 122:1)

How do you feel about going to church every Sunday? The psalmist indicates an enthusiasm for worship. The early Christians also gladly met daily in homes and at least weekly to worship. An every-Sunday glad!

Unfortunately, we sometimes lack the joy of worship. Why? First of all, we may subconsciously say, "I was *afraid* when they said to me, 'Let us go to the house of the Lord.'" We may be afraid to come because we haven't kept up with our church pledge. We feel unworthy. We come because we feel duty-bound. We want to avoid hell or excommunication from the Church. No gladness in worship when we are afraid.

Second, we may be saying, "I was *stubborn* when they said to me, 'Let us go to the house of the Lord.' No one can tell me what to do. I live in a free country. I'm not coming to church until I feel like it!" No gladness in worship when we are stubborn.

Third, we could be saying, "I was *bored* when they said to me, 'Let us go to the house of the Lord.' Other things excite me more, such as golf, camping, or even sleeping. I'm bored at church—the same old service and the same kind of sermons." No gladness in worship when we are bored.

Only God can give us an every-Sunday gladness. He sent His Son for us with a life of glad worship. The temple of His body, though destroyed, was raised up on the third day. He stands at the center of His people with His blood-bought forgiveness. God transforms our hearts through faith in His promises. His Word and Sacraments cleanse us of fear, stubbornness, and boredom. We come together into His presence with high expectations. Silent before Him, we hear again of His love. He fills ours hearts with gladness that endures.

A MOUTHFUL

> My mouth is filled with Your praise, and with
> Your glory all the day.
> (Psalm 71:8)

Picture a delightful, tasty morsel filling your mouth—a juicy filet mignon, a tangy lemon meringue pie with flaky crust, or a superb pasta with zesty meat sauce. What a mouthful to be savored and then swallowed with delight. Nevertheless, before long, the stomach grows full and the appetite wanes.

The psalmist describes a different kind of mouthful, no less delightful: "My mouth is filled with Your praise, and with Your glory all the day." Struggling with evil around him, needing deliverance from the grasp of wicked and cruel men, he nevertheless remembers the marvelous blessings of God from the moment of his birth. He sees God as his hope, refuge, and rescue. Therefore his mouth is filled with God's praise, not just for a hungry moment, but all day long. The more he declares the splendor of God, the more he enjoys his mouthful of praise.

What about us? Do we fill our mouth only with fattening foods? Do we fill our mouth with complaining, profaning, or slandering words all day long? Or can we say with the psalmist, "My mouth is filled with Your praise, and with Your glory all the day"?

How often our indulgent mouthfuls turn flat and indigestion follows. How often our negative words leave our mouths stale and empty, with an emotional hangover remaining.

God spoke His joyful word at creation, at Bethlehem, at Jordan, and at the empty tomb. He still speaks at the baptismal font, the lectern, and the altar that our sins are forgiven as we eat Christ's body and drink His blood. Indeed, by His grace—from birth to death and beyond—the Holy Spirit fills our mouth with His praise all day long. What a mouthful!

THE JOY OF TOGETHERNESS

I thank my God in all my remembrance of you, always in every prayer of mine for you all making my prayer with joy, because of your partnership in the gospel from the first day until now. (Philippians 1:3–5)

Paul rejoices at his close relationship with the Philippian believers and at their relationship with God their Father and the Lord Jesus Christ. That partnership in the Gospel brings joy when he is with them and even when he is physically separated from them as a prisoner. He knows the joy of togetherness.

Over the years, I have led and participated in many groups that gathered around the Word of Christ. Some were informal, for example, when we vacationed together. Some were short term for a weekend retreat, a few weeks, or months. On occasions, I visited with a Bible breakfast group only once or twice. Others were long term with the continuity of several years. God's Spirit worked through the Word in every instance.

Often, as people became better acquainted, prayer life grew and personal sharing from God's Word took on a greater honesty and caring for one another. Certainly, we helped one another and sought strength from God's Word in difficult times. What stands out in my mind is laughter together, expressions of thanksgiving to God for His blessings, and spontaneous encouragement from the Word of Christ. We enjoyed being together. We enjoyed the study of God's Word and its application to our lives. We enjoyed the prayer time. We enjoyed getting together informally at other times for Christian fellowship. "Rejoice in the Lord always; again I will say, Rejoice" (Philippians 4:4).

THE JOY OF GIVING

One of my greatest joys has always been the privilege of giving to others a Scripture verse at a time of need. When the Word of Christ speaks to our hearts, we want to share with those we love. Scripture came alive for me when I visited a hospital patient, a homebound elderly person, or someone coming for counsel because of a personal or marital problem.

I vividly remember visiting my mother in the hospital shortly before her death in August 1979. After working full time well into her seventies, Mom was diagnosed with inoperable breast cancer and would die of a major stroke in a few days. How would I reach out to her, show her my love, and bring God's comfort to her heart? A Scripture verse popped into my mind from the book of Isaiah. Immediately, I knew that for a worrier such as me, this verse would convey God's message. I quoted from the King James Version of the Bible: "Thou wilt keep him in perfect peace, whose mind is stayed on Thee: because he trusteth in Thee" (Isaiah 26:3 KJV).

I took her hands in mine and prayed for the peace of God, which passes all understanding through faith in Christ Jesus. Through my tears, I experienced the joy of giving my mom the Word of Christ.

THE JOY OF TIMELINESS

Over the years, my heart has rejoiced at God's Word because the Holy Spirit has a perfect sense of timing. When I read five psalms and one chapter of Proverbs each day, I frequently find one or two verses that seem perfect for my current situation, speaking to my heart, sometimes exposing my sins, sometimes offering powerful comfort, sometimes guiding my day. I place a date by the verse and make a brief note. Over the years, I have filled several different Bibles with marginal notations. My joy comes with the timeliness of God's Word.

Recently, God's timeliness demonstrated itself through a devotion I had written for a Lenten series almost a year previously. The topic was "Seismic Shocks," and it was read on the Friday after Ash Wednesday, March 11, 2011, the very day that a devastating earthquake and tsunami struck Japan. The Scripture verse chosen was Psalm 60:2: "You have made the land to quake; You have torn it open; repair its breaches, for it totters." I received many phone calls regarding the timeliness of the devotion, which was totally the Spirit's work, not mine. I rejoice in God's timely Word for our salvation.

THE JOY OF DISCOVERY

The adventure will continue in the next section, "Living Deeply in the Word of Christ." Hopefully, you are discovering more and more of the Word of Christ as you taste it in many settings and see that the Lord is good. God has many discoveries in mind for you.

Our LifeLight community finds the study of 1 and 2 Peter more meaningful because we studied Isaiah first. We are discovering how often Peter builds on Isaiah and quotes it directly. Last Sunday evening, our home Bible study group was nearing the end of a study on Revelation. I was amazed to discover that Revelation 18 echoes Isaiah's prophecy against Tyre. These are small examples of the joy of discovery. I have selected the Bible sections quoted in this book as God opens up new connections for me in His Word. They bear careful reading in the context of living with passion in the Word of Christ. Open your life to His Word, and fasten your seat belts as the adventure continues. "Rejoice in the Lord always; again I will say, Rejoice" (Philippians 4:4).

PART FIVE

LIVING DEEPLY IN
THE WORD OF CHRIST

> But as for you, continue in what you have
> learned and have firmly believed, knowing
> from whom you learned it and how from
> childhood you have been acquainted with
> the sacred writings, which are able to make
> you wise for salvation through faith in Christ
> Jesus. All Scripture is breathed out by God
> and profitable for teaching, for reproof, for
> correction, and for training in righteousness,
> that the man of God may be competent,
> equipped for every good work.
> (2 Timothy 3:14–17)

Paul encourages the young pastor Timothy to continue in the
Scripture. Certainly Timothy had discovered the prophetic
writings as a child from his grandmother Lois and mother
Eunice (2 Timothy 1:5), but now he learns more and more about
his salvation through faith in Christ Jesus and applies all of the
inspired Scripture to his own life and ministry as learner and
teacher. Through this immersion in God's Word, Timothy's
heart beats as one with God's heart. He lives with God's passion
for the Church and for the world.

This part of *Heartbeat!* moves us deeper into the Word of
Christ. By the Spirit's power, we never stop craving spiritual milk
like newborn babies. Yet we seek to eat a steady diet of solid food,
which prepares us for the spiritual warfare we face and for all the
opportunities to share Christ with others. God leads us to embrace

Christ-help in every circumstance as we live deeply in His Word. That in-depth immersion in the Word enables us to grow in our faith through testing of many kinds, and that testing drives us deeper into the Word, which transforms lives, including our own, and shapes a biblical worldview in which our heart beats in rhythm with God's heart of compassion for the world.

Craving Spiritual Milk

> Like newborn babies, crave pure spiritual
> milk, so that by it you may grow up in your
> salvation. (1 Peter 2:2 NIV)

At first, you might think it strange to begin a major part of this book—a part titled "Living Deeply in the Word of Christ"—with a Scripture verse on babies craving milk. Should this part not be addressing us as adults with significant education and experience? The question reveals the problem. Peter's audience consisted of adult believers, some of Jewish background, with knowledge of the Hebrew Scriptures, and some of Gentile background, coming from a pagan world. Apparently both groups needed to crave pure spiritual milk like babies.

God's Word has no lack of depth or staying power. Peter has just reminded them that they had been born again, "not of perishable seed but of imperishable, through the living and abiding word of God" (1 Peter 1:23). The Word of God is shallow enough for a child to wade in and deep enough for an elephant to drown in. No human being will ever master the Word of the Lord, which remains forever (1 Peter 1:25). Whether young or old, human beings often rely on themselves for knowledge and experience, thus rejecting or ignoring the Word of Christ. They end up like flowers that fade and grass that withers. Their lack of craving for God's Good News shows in their lifestyle of "malice and all deceit and hypocrisy and envy and all slander" (1 Peter 2:1). The result of craving pure spiritual milk is actually spiritual growth and maturity: "Like newborn babies, crave pure spiritual milk, so that by it you may grow up in your salvation, now that you have tasted that the Lord is good" (1 Peter 2:2–3 NIV). Apply these thoughts about craving to your weekly spiritual walk.

CRAVING SPIRITUAL MILK

People yawn in the pews waiting for the termination of the sermon. We complain, "Do we have to read family devotions again? I've got homework and a great television program to watch." "I wanted to read my Bible this morning, but I just couldn't get up." How can we persuade one another to read and hear the Word of God?

How much persuasion does a hungry baby need to drink milk? The crying baby grabs hold and eagerly drinks the milk until satisfied. Then, contentedly, the baby relaxes and goes to sleep. "Craving milk" is Peter's expression: he has already explained that we are born again through the living and abiding Word of God. Everything else withers and fades away, "but the word of the Lord remains forever" (1 Peter 1:25). That Word tells of the death and resurrection of Jesus Christ to bring us a living hope and a secure inheritance. Pure spiritual milk indeed!

Craving, you say? Not yawning, enduring, or complaining, but craving? Yes, craving pure spiritual milk. Hungry first. There is no pure spiritual milk in the world. Malice, deceit, hypocrisy, envy, and slander, but no spiritual milk. We try to make it on our own without drinking God's pure spiritual milk, but we only begin to fret and cry. Finally, we feel the gnawing of inner hunger. No one can hold us, cradle us, and rock us enough to satisfy that hunger.

Close to the pure spiritual milk, we get all excited. We crave it. We grab hold and eagerly drink the Word of Christ's love for us and drink and drink and drink. Contentedly, we fall asleep in the quiet confidence that more pure spiritual milk awaits us on the morrow.

God's Spirit creates in us the craving for pure spiritual milk. He uses the daily battle for survival in a competitive, hostile world to drain and exhaust us. He uses our futile efforts to seek the wrong kind of spiritual food and drink—success, wealth, popularity, phony religions—to leave us empty and unfulfilled. Then, when we are desperately hungry and thirsty, He leads us to long for salvation, hunger for the Bread of Life, thirst for the Living Water, and, yes, crave the pure spiritual milk of His Word. Apply these words to a current struggle you are enduring.

THROUGH A GLASS WINDOW AT CHURCH

My soul longs for Your salvation;
I hope in Your word. (Psalm 119:81)

The other Sunday morning, our family arrived late for the 9:15 service at church. Already somewhat in turmoil because of the last-minute rush, we found ourselves sitting on chairs in the overflow area looking through a glass window. The service proceeded. We strained to hear. We longed to participate and find nourishment in the Word of God, but only snatches of the readings and the sermon drifted through.

Growing frustration welled up within me. I needed God's peace and assurance, His guidance and direction. I needed to confess my animosity toward the family for making me late and to explain to them why the worship hour on Sunday meant so much to me. I realized how cut off I felt from the congregation at worship.

And I needed to hear God's word of absolution—His forgiveness for those sins!

Perhaps the psalmist experienced similar feelings when he wrote, "My soul longs for Your salvation" (Psalm 119:81 NIV). He felt cut off from God's presence as others persecuted him, and his suffering continued. Nevertheless, he added the words, "I hope in Your word" (verse 81 NIV). He knew that God had promised salvation through the coming of the Messiah.

Our family learned a lesson that Sunday through the glass window at church. We discovered how easily we can take hearing God's Word for granted. Distraught in our late arrival and frustrated by our straining to hear, we fainted with longing for God's salvation. In the car on the way home and at the Sunday dinner table, we put our hope in God's Word. We confessed to one another our wrong words and actions. We shared our need for regular growth in God's Word. Most of all, we looked to Jesus Christ, our Savior and friend, who graced our dinner and even our discouraging hour in the overflow area. We can always see and hear Him, even through a glass window at church.

My simple prayer forty years ago, "Lord, give me a thirst for Your Word," was not a one-time craving for pure spiritual milk. God did answer my prayer almost immediately. I read and read each day, delighted to discover many wonderful truths in the first weeks. By God's grace, the craving has continued. I have experienced many dry periods when the Word did not seem to speak to my needs or touch my heart: my fault, not His. Yet God's Spirit always leads me to thirst and crave. I want more of God and His plan for the world and His assurance of forgiveness and salvation. That Spirit-worked craving brings me deeper into the Word of Christ.

Pray for that craving, not only today but also next week and next month. Expect God's Spirit to create that craving in you. He will satisfy you with the pure spiritual milk of the Word of Christ. Your spiritual heart will beat faster with God's passion for living out your calling today, but it will also beat steadily and strongly for your deeper immersion in that Word

Eating a Steady
Diet of Solid Food

> But solid food is for the mature, for those who
> have their powers of discernment trained by
> constant practice to distinguish good from evil.
> (Hebrews 5:14)

How large a part does the study of God's Word play in your daily life? Do you spend time with the Scripture readings used in the Sunday worship service, before or afterwards? Do you engage in some group study of those passages? Do you have daily personal or family readings of Scripture, perhaps as part of devotional reading and prayer? Do you or have you followed some systematic plan for reading the entire Bible in one or two years? For example, *Today's Light Bible* (Concordia Publishing House: St. Louis, 1999) helps you read through the Bible in two years, and it provides brief devotional thoughts for each day. Do you interact with your Bible reading by marking or underlining as you read meaningful passages, by praying as you read, or by writing the date and making a brief note in the margin as God's Word speaks to you in a helpful manner for your life at that moment? Have you engaged in an in-depth study of individual books of the Bible? The LifeLight series, published by Concordia Publishing House, offers the opportunity to join fellow believers

HEARTBEAT!: Living with Passion in the Word of Christ

in a format of individual study aided by a study guide, small-group weekly discussion of that individual study, and a summary lecture of the material for that week. Have you participated in survey courses of the Bible, helping you to integrate biblical themes throughout Scripture, presenting God's plan of salvation from eternity to Christ's second coming?

These questions barely scratch the surface of what it might mean for you to move from drinking spiritual milk to eating a steady diet of solid spiritual food. The Church's ancient Collect for the Word grasps the essence of growing to spiritual maturity in the Word of Christ:

> Blessed Lord, You have caused all Holy Scriptures to be written for our learning. Grant that we may so hear them, read, mark, learn, and inwardly digest them that, by patience and comfort of Your holy Word, we may embrace and ever hold fast the blessed hope of everlasting life; through Jesus Christ, our Lord. (*Lutheran Service Book,* p. 308)

Your life in this twenty-first-century world presents significant challenges to your faith and practical daily life of service and witness. The devil prowls around like a roaring lion seeking to devour you (1 Peter 5:8). Temptations to sin lurk around every corner as the words and images of the world appeal to your sinful flesh. You are engaged in spiritual warfare, which threatens to lead you into apostasy. In that context, the writer to the Hebrews writes:

> About this we have much to say, and it is hard to explain, since you have become dull of hearing. For though by this time you ought to be teachers, you need someone to teach you again the basic principles of the oracles of God. You need milk, not solid food, for everyone who lives on milk is unskilled in the

word of righteousness, since he is a child.

But solid food is for the mature, for those who have their powers of discernment trained by constant practice to distinguish good from evil. (Hebrews 5:11–14)

These words are addressed to you and to me, wherever you might be in the process of Christian maturity. Remember: God is the one who shapes us by His Word. The more we open that Word, "hear them, read, mark, learn, and inwardly digest" the Word of Christ, the more God's Spirit points us to Christ our Savior and helps us grow in the faith. He transforms us daily and over a lifetime of experiences to reflect Christ's forgiveness in our lives. Why not start today or tomorrow in God's Word and let God's Spirit deepen your daily walk?

DAILY AT THE DOOR

Blessed is the one who listens to me, watching daily at my gates, waiting beside my doors. (Proverbs 8:34)

Many successful people started out at the doorstep of those they admired. Many children in American history came to the doors of printers, blacksmiths, and bakers to apprentice themselves for a career. Young men followed Socrates and other philosophers to gain morsels of wisdom.

Proverbs 8 personifies Wisdom and declares, "Whoever finds me finds life and obtains favor from the LORD" (verse 35). Pride and arrogance stand condemned. Evil behavior and perverse speech are hated. Simple, humble willingness to come to God and let Him guide into all truth brings wisdom. Waiting daily at the door of God's wisdom brings life.

Today's world provides many competing doorsteps: scientific knowledge, business acumen, psychological success strategies, and secular philosophies. Each beckons from a daily visit at the door. Wisdom's door as described by Proverbs may appear less appealing.

However, that wisdom leads to Christ, the power of God and the wisdom of God. Try reading Proverbs 8, substituting Christ for wisdom and its pronouns. Wait at the door of Bethlehem, the temple, the Nazareth synagogue, the home of Mary and Martha, the Upper Room. Follow Him on the dusty roads, along the seashore, through the Jerusalem streets to Calvary, to the mountain in Galilee. Read the Word. Worship in His house with bread and wine. Being daily at the door—His Word—means life, eternal life, for you and for those you bring to Him.

For me, it all starts daily: a need to confess sins and rejoice at God's forgiveness for facing the new day, the baptismal life. I open the Word expectantly and prayerfully as I read five psalms and one chapter of Proverbs. I underline, pause to reflect and pray, write a note in the margins, and add today's date. I notice other dates and marginal notes from previous months and years. My wife and I sit at the breakfast table, read some devotion based on Scripture, and spend time in prayer, each day based on the theme or specific needs of others for prayer. Sometimes I write in a journal what God has been teaching me through His Word and recent experiences. Currently, I only write in the journal every few months. At other times of particular stress or challenges, I write more frequently, even daily. When Gail and I prepare for LifeLight or reflect on the weekly group gathering, we often share what God has taught us. We have similar discussions after weekly worship. We also take note of witness opportunities during the week and evidences of how God is working in people's lives, for which we give thanks.

We confess failed opportunities, lack of boldness for witness, and obstacles to receiving His Word in our hearts. How we need God's love and forgiveness and His discernment for guiding our lives!

Hebrews suggests constant use of the solid food of God's Word as we train ourselves to distinguish good from evil. God sent His Son to die for our immaturities. He opens up the Word for us with its forgiveness and nurturing power. As we attend to that Word, we receive the nourishment necessary for growth. That steady diet of solid food produces deeper insights and a dynamic life of service. God's heart beats steadily and passionately in our hearts!

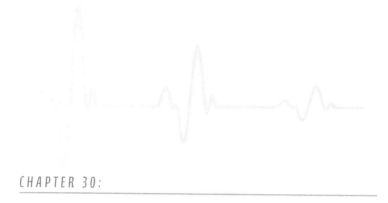

Embracing
Christ-Help

> I have been crucified with Christ. It is no
> longer I who live, but Christ who lives in me.
> And the life I now live in the flesh I live by
> faith in the Son of God, who loved me and
> gave Himself for me. (Galatians 2:20)

> For in Christ Jesus you are all sons of God,
> through faith. For as many of you as were
> baptized into Christ have put on Christ.
> (Galatians 3:26–27)

In Galatians, the apostle Paul renounces self-help, relying on the
works of the Law, either for justification or for the daily Christian
life, and embraces "faith working through love" (Galatians 5:6)
as we "walk by the Spirit" (5:25). He clearly embraces Christ-
help—Christ *for* him on Calvary and Christ *in* him through
Baptism (2:20; 3:26–27). He then urges the Galatian believers
and us to embrace Christ-help in the freedom of serving one
another through love (5:13).

Living deeply in the Word of Christ not only leads us to crave
spiritual milk again and again and to eat a steady diet of solid spiritual food but also to embrace Christ-help for our daily walk in

this world. With Paul we confess, "It is no longer I who live, but Christ who lives in me. And the life I now live in the flesh I live by faith in the Son of God, who loved me and gave Himself for me" (Galatians 2:20).

Picture one week of your life. Include all of your responsibilities at home, at work, and in your leisure time. Be as specific as you can regarding the details in each arena of your life. Ask yourself what difference it would make to embrace Christ-help instead of self-help in specific situations. Where have you found help from Scripture and prayer to face these situations? What self-help efforts have led to failure and a need to confess sins? How have you been helped by encouragement coming from brothers and sisters in Christ? Consider the power from God available to you as you embrace Christ-help.

POWER SOURCE UNLIMITED

> That you may know . . . what is the
> immeasurable greatness of His power toward
> us who believe. (Ephesians 1:18b–19a)

Today our world knows limits. We need tremendous power every day to drive industrial machines, light cities and homes, fuel cars, and heat buildings. What power sources can we find? Power is in great demand. Power sources are limited.

How exciting are the words of Paul in the spiritual realm! Writing to the Ephesians, Paul describes a power source unlimited: "What is the immeasurable greatness of His power toward us who believe, according to the working of His great might that He worked in Christ when He raised Him from the dead and seated Him at His right hand in the heavenly places" (Ephesians 1:19–20).

We have power for Christian living: God's power. He demonstrated that power by raising Christ from the dead. The resurrection powerfully announces God's acceptance of Christ's sacrifice for our sins. Weak and helpless on our own, inept to help others, we receive God's power when He works faith in our hearts at our Baptism. In short, Christ's resurrection power becomes available "toward us who believe." Christ continues to reign in power at the right hand of the Father. Therefore, plugged into Christ by faith, we possess a power source unlimited. What a comfort to know that God's spiritual power source will never run low!

WORD POWER

> For I am not ashamed of the gospel, for it is the power of God for salvation to everyone who believes. (Romans 1:16)

Dynamite packs terrific power. Atomic and hydrogen bombs contain terrifying power. Modern technology sports an impressive array of powerful machines. However, words perhaps convey even greater power. A word triggers the dynamite in the bombs and instructs powerful machines to operate.

We looked at God's spiritual power source unlimited, focusing on the resurrection of Jesus Christ from the dead. Romans 1:16, our text, describes the Word that unlocks that power source.

Gospel—the Word. Good news. God's Good News about a Savior who took upon Himself our unrighteousness. Righteous. He paid the price on the cross. God declares the world righteous for Christ's sake. That righteousness comes to us by faith in Christ.

Paul calls that Gospel the power of God for salvation, "dynamite" according to the Greek word for power. Word power. Gospel power. The Church preaches that Word and administers the Sacraments as visible words.

We hear the Gospel every day for our own assurance and power. We speak the Gospel every day for the salvation of others. We live the Gospel. Word power unlocks God's spiritual power source unlimited.

GO POWER

All authority in heaven and on earth has been given to Me. Go therefore and make disciples of all nations. (Matthew 28:18–19a)

America: a nation on the go. We work, travel, exercise, play, and celebrate. We get up early, work through lunch, and stay up late. We live by the clock and the digital watch and the odometer. We need "go power" to keep moving—breakfast cereals, fruit juices, vitamins, candy bars, and pep pills. Nevertheless, we frequently run out of gas and lie exhausted in front of the television.

Most of us would agree that some of this going makes little sense. There is one going, however, that is of the utmost importance. Jesus speaks of it to His disciples for the sake of His church when He says, "Go therefore and make disciples of all nations, baptizing them in the name of the Father and of the Son and of the Holy Spirit, teaching them to observe all that I have commanded you" (Matthew 28:19–20). Not going to get rich or to find thrills, but going to make disciples of all nations, to share that Gospel Word power as part of God's Church with family members, neighbors, co-workers, golfing partners, church friends, and people in other lands. Good reason for going.

Where do we get the power for such going? Jesus answers that question on the Great Commission mountain. "All authority in heaven and on earth has been given to Me," He says. He supplies the go power from His limitless supply. Crucified and risen from the dead, He offers forgiveness and endless refreshment. Through

Word power—His Gospel—we receive all the go power we will ever need. He promises to be with us always, to the very end of the age. What comfort!

STAYING POWER

> But He said to me, "My grace is sufficient for you, for My power is made perfect in weakness." (2 Corinthians 12:9)

True power needs to last. Many distance runners start with a burst of energy but fade on the stretch. The best athletes sometimes lose to a steadier team, which takes better conditioning into the final quarter or overtime period. We are describing staying power.

God provides His Word, which brings us the crucified and risen Savior. He intends for us to use His resources to keep going over the long haul, to have staying power.

Paul, the great on-the-go missionary, learned the importance of staying power when God sent him a thorn in the flesh, some illness or physical handicap that simply wouldn't go away. Paul prayed and hoped, but the problem remained. Discouraged and frustrated, Paul finally got the message of our text. Paul was being conditioned for the long haul. He felt weak and unable to continue. At that point, he learned to accept his weakness and rely totally on God's grace and power. Now he could face any troubles, because Christ was always there for him.

Similarly, we will experience discouragement and frustration after our initial going. We will experience God's testing in our personal lives as well as in our witnessing efforts. God says also to us, "My grace is sufficient for you, for My power is made perfect in weakness." We look to the weak and helpless Son of God, nailed to a cross for us, and then experience His resurrection power flowing from the empty tomb to us in our weakness.

Consider Christian people in your life who seem to live with a quiet confidence, joyful energy, humility, and constant concern for others. They may also share their faith in Christ naturally. In my growing up years, I remember a scoutmaster, a youth leader, a high school basketball coach, and a professor who radiated their faith in Christ. In totally different ways, they influenced my walk with the Lord.

In more recent years, I learned to embrace Christ-help through my father-in-law, a family counselor colleague, a beloved pastor friend, my wife, and my own children. Together we discover what it means to embrace Christ-help as we live the baptismal life. God's heart beats in the Christian community gathered around Word and Sacraments and in our own hearts!

Growing through Testing

> Beloved, do not be surprised at the fiery trial
> when it comes upon you to test you, as though
> something strange were happening to you. But
> rejoice insofar as you share Christ's sufferings,
> that you may also rejoice and be glad when His
> glory is revealed. (1 Peter 4:12–13)

Most of Part 4, "Living Deeply in the Word of Christ," has focused on strengthening our spiritual heartbeat with regular use of God's Word in our lives—personal and family devotional life, weekly worship, and group Bible study in a variety of settings. God's Spirit leads us to crave spiritual milk, eat a steady diet of solid food, and embrace Christ-help daily and throughout our lives.

This chapter introduces the spiritual growth God can bring when we face times of testing. Scripture is full of examples: Joseph in Egypt; Moses before Pharaoh, at the Red Sea, and in the wilderness; Joshua moving across the Jordan into the Promised Land; David in one crisis after another; Jesus' disciples at the time of His death and later in the Early Church after Pentecost. Peter writes to various branches of the Church in Asia Minor that they should not be surprised when the fiery trial of persecution tests their faith. Christ suffered for them and us as He "bore our sins in His body on the tree" (1 Peter 2:24), and we can expect suffering for the sake of Christ as we follow His example. The early believers grew in faith and in boldness to live for Christ through these times of testing.

In what ways has your faith been tested in your life? Struggles at work, major family problems, serious illness, or the death of loved ones can bring us to our knees. Standing up for our faith in Christ when others ridicule or abuse us also puts us to the test. In those times of testing, how has God brought you strength and comfort? Has He provided a caring Christian friend with a timely Scripture verse, the prayers of many on your behalf, or a sermon or Bible study meant just for you? Have you been drawn more deeply into the Word of Christ just because you are being tested? Can you now look back and see how your faith has grown, how your heart beats stronger spiritually because of that time of testing?

Earlier in this book, I made reference to a major time of testing in our family, the three-and-a-half year illness and death of our daughter Becky in January 1993, at the age of 23. I would like to describe how God sustained us through this painful period and helped us grow in the Word of Christ so that we might better live with passion for Christ. First, I will share some words from the journal I wrote daily when we joined Becky in Seattle for her bone marrow transplant. Next, I will include words from our daughter Amy, which she spoke to a group of young mothers ten years after Becky's death.

REFLECTIONS ON REBECCA
MONDAY, DECEMBER 14, 1992

I begin this account in the middle of things. Becky lies in the adjoining room (SW 1009) at Swedish Hospital Medical Center in Seattle. She has just begun receiving radical chemotherapy (Cytoxan) in preparation for her bone marrow transplant on Friday, December 18, 1992. She is experiencing nausea and sleeping a great deal. Gail sits at my side in the day room as we look out over the Seattle skyline at Puget Sound and a ferry heading for Bremerton or Bainbridge Island. The skies are overcast with a light drizzle falling on this December morning. I can see the Space Needle at the Seattle Center, where a few nights ago, Becky and her fiancé, Greg Haecker, Gail, and I ate dinner in the Emerald Suite, a revolving restaurant near the top. I can also see the Kingdome, where two weeks ago Becky and I saw the Seattle Seahawks-Denver Broncos football game. We celebrated and enjoyed life during those outpatient days at the Fred Hutchinson Cancer Research Center, where Becky underwent tests and conferences in preparation for the transplant.

We Carters have been on a three-and-a-half-year journey that began in July 1989, when Becky was found to have low blood counts and was later diagnosed as having aplastic anemia, a disease of the bone marrow. The journey has led through many crisis situations and emotional upheavals as well as many learning experiences and overwhelming manifestations of the love and grace of God, to the present moment, when life hangs in the balance and the hope of healing beats strong.

Many journeys swirl in my mind as images of Becky's current journey toward healing. I think of Abraham taking his son, his only son, Isaac, at God's command on that journey to Mount Moriah. That image has been on my mind for over three years and was recalled by a reference to the passage in a phone call from Dean Wenthe on Saturday, December 12. God provided a ram for the sacrifice. How will God provide a ram for the Carter family? We pray that the bone marrow donor will be that ram.

The journey of Israel across the Red Sea, through the wilderness, and to the Promised Land also provides a parallel for our days and weeks and years, now hours.

Over the past weeks, I have pondered the relationship of a bone marrow transplant to the birth of Jesus Christ, the incarnation, and our new life in Holy Baptism. A birth brings new life into the world. A bone marrow transplant brings new life to the very core of a person's being. "Life is in the blood" (see Leviticus 17:11). "O holy Child of Bethlehem, Descend to us, we pray; Cast out our sin, and enter in, Be born in us today" (*LSB* 361:4). If, in fact, this relationship exists, then we journey with Mary and Joseph, the shepherds, and the Wise Men to Bethlehem this Christmas in a new light. The journey toward healing takes on added depth. "Mary kept all these things and pondered them in her heart" (see Luke 2:19). She experienced the Christ Child growing within her, knew the problems and hurts caused by public opinion, endured the pain of childbirth, and rejoiced quietly at the birth of the Savior and the adoring worship of shepherds and Magi. Becky experiences the growing bone marrow depletion, knows the problems and hurts caused by the treatments and effects of the disease, endures the pain of chemotherapy and a transplant, and prepares to rejoice quietly at the new bone marrow bringing life, as all those Christian friends and family members praise God for His miraculous healing.

In a lesser way, our journey by auto to Seattle symbolizes our journey toward healing. We spent four days on the road, driving though all sorts of weather with a packed car. We drove through heavy snow near Denver, Salt Lake City, and Pendleton, Oregon, but also rejoiced in a sunny drive through the Columbia River Gorge.

FRIDAY, DECEMBER 18, 1992 —TRANSPLANT DAY—3:00 P.M.

Christmas is in the air, but not because of seasonal decorations and trappings. It's because Becky will receive the precious gift of bone marrow from an anonymous donor within the next couple of hours. New life. New hope. A rebirth of sorts. Just like, in a small measure, the first Christmas, when God's Son was born to bring new life to the world. The bone marrow will come quietly in a pouch, looking for all the world like a blood transfusion or another IV medication, but it brings the hope of new blood cells produced throughout a lifetime from healthy marrow in Becky's body. The old must go. The new will come. God's Son came quietly in the still of the night in a humble manger located in the little town of Bethlehem, but His birth brought the hope of salvation for the world, worked out in His sinless life under the Law, His sacrificial death on the cross, and His triumphant resurrection from the grave. We will remain thankful for the gift of the donor who doesn't even know our daughter but who is willing to sacrifice on her behalf by submitting to a surgical procedure to share his own bone marrow with her. We will begin counting the days post-transplant, waiting for good news that the new bone marrow is engrafted and producing healthy blood cells. As the psalmist says, "I wait for the LORD, my soul does wait, and in His Word do I hope. I wait for the Lord more than they that watch for the morning. I say, more than they that watch for the morning. (see Psalm 130:5–6). We heed the further word of the psalmist: "O Israel, put your hope in the LORD, for with the LORD is unfailing love and with Him is full redemption" (see verse 7).

As we have been waiting for the bone marrow to arrive, Chaplain John Luthans visited to share with us (Gail and I, Greg, Becky's friend Kim, and, of course, Becky) a word from Scripture. He chose the very same psalm I had planned to share with Becky, Psalm 139, parts of which he read from *The Living Bible.*

Today has been a clear, sunny day overlooking Puget Sound. I see the sun beginning to set in the west as I view downtown Seattle preparing for Christmas. The malls are open and busy. Soon the light of Christmas will again illumine the city. A few patches of Wednesday night's snow remain on the ground. The sentiment of Christmas is everywhere. Nowhere does that feeling have more depth for the Carter family than in room 1009 of Swedish Hospital where, for Becky Carter, a most wonderful Christmas present is coming exactly one week early, December 18, 1992.

FRIDAY, DECEMBER 25, 1992 —CHRISTMAS DAY—TRANSPLANT + 7

I'm writing these thoughts around 5:00 p.m. Many images and experiences fill my senses. The Christmas Eve service last night at Trinity closed with a unique candle-lighting ceremony. The whole congregation left the pews and made a circle around the nave. With the lights out, we faced the cross and sang "Beautiful Savior," followed by the lighting of the candles, the Lord's Prayer, and the singing of "Silent Night." As we faced one another with lit candles, I suddenly understood the meaning of the Body of Christ. I pictured Becky in the middle of the congregation, lifted up by prayers from around the country: Dave Ludwig in Hickory, North Carolina; Bruce and Dottie Rudolf in Patchogue, Long Island, New York; Paul Schroeder and the Haeckers in Wisconsin; Randy Shields in Ann Arbor; Don Luepke, Dean Wenthe, Sue Hebel, and Gene and Donna Brunow in Fort Wayne; the Rabers, Von Hadens, and Phil Krupske in Peru, Indiana; Alan Harre, the Feltens, and Warren Rubel in Valpo; Gene Krentz, Pam Heisler, and Greg's friends in the Chicago area; the Englebrechts and John Luthans in Seattle; Norb and Jackie Oesch in Orange, California; and Jack Gerber, Herb Hinsch, Luther Brunette, and those at Salem in St. Louis. These as well as hundreds of others, worshiping the newborn Savior and praying for Becky. We all wept during that ceremony—light in darkness indeed.

All the while, Becky struggles—continued bleeding and platelet problems, perhaps peptic ulcers to go with mild veno-occlusive disease, too many fluids retained in her body, much tiredness, consistent pain. She roused a bit last evening for some Christmas visiting and again this morning for opening Christmas presents. Because she needed an x-ray, she got to leave the LAF room in her sterile garb and got to walk once around the hallway. A small victory of sorts.

We picked up Mark and Kayla at the airport yesterday morning before I gave platelets. They have been joining in the hospital visits, church services, and so on. Amy is a trooper and loyally spends as much time as possible at the hospital.

SATURDAY, JANUARY 9, 1993— TRANSPLANT + 22

As I write in the day room before morning rounds, Becky lies in grave condition. This morning they had to intubate her, which means she is under sedation and on a breathing machine. Her BUN, creatinine, and bilirubin counts are rising. She is bleeding somewhere internally and thus needs blood product to keep up her hematocrit. Greg stayed all night and is hurting and exhausted.

I feel a peace inside—not of my own doing, because I am desperately wanting Becky's healing—but of God's making. His Spirit is working in Becky and in us. She is in God's hands. He loves her and us. I want her healing, marriage, and a life of service. I want God to be glorified in her life and ours. I pray for the faith of all the people who are praying and love Becky. And I pray for God to work a miracle by healing her. "Nothing in my hand I bring; Simply to Thy cross I cling" (*LSB* 761:3).

Three and a half years all come down to these crisis hours. Guide the doctors and the medications. Let all of Becky's inner strength and resources be released to aid the healing process. Keep our faith strong as we rely totally on Your healing mercies. You are strong and You are loving. You have a perfect plan for Becky's earthly life here and her eternal life in heaven. The same thing applies to Greg and the rest of our family.

Becky died around 3:30 or 4:00 p.m. During the day, they had trouble keeping up her blood hematocrit because of internal bleeding somewhere. Suddenly, around 3:00, a massive bleeding in the brain destroyed all functions, including the brain stem cell. We watched her die peacefully as they disconnected the ventilating machine, and we were able to spend some time with her afterward.

SUNDAY, JANUARY 10, 1993

As I write this, Gail and I are winging our way over Montana on the way to St. Louis, where Herb Hinsch will meet us at the airport. Greg's brother Mark arrived from Orlando last night, and they got a 1:00 a.m. flight for Chicago. Our Mark will fly to Minneapolis this afternoon.

We are filled with emotion; not much sleep last night after busy packing, many tears, and mutual hugs, but we rejoice for Becky and see God's plan for her and for us through the tears—God's plans—not to harm but to prosper, for hope and a future. I want to help two things happen: some type of ongoing memorial funding at both Concordia Lutheran High School and Valparaiso University in Becky's honor, and some way of telling her story and the impact of her life and illness on the lives of many people and many churches who prayed for us and supported us.

Gail and I want to stay close through this tragedy, keep our family close, and also reach out to Greg.

AMY SCHULTZ'S WITNESS, 2003

It was January 9, 1993. My husband, Joel, had just been a groomsman in a friend's wedding, and we were coming home late at night. I always check the answering machine for messages when we get home, and the light was blinking on this night. There was one message, from my father, saying, "Call us tonight, no matter what time you get home." Knowing how important sleep was to my parents, I knew something was very wrong.

This was a phone call I will never forget. Dad's words were simple but devastating. "Becky died tonight." The only words I had were shouted at my father, "No, no, no!" Over and over I said them until I couldn't anymore. We cried over the phone together, Joel held me, we said our good-byes, and then I was just numb. How could this have happened?

You see, my twenty-three-year-old sister, Becky, was in Fred Hutchinson Cancer Center in Seattle, Washington, where she had just received a bone marrow transplant in December. She had been battling aplastic anemia, a blood disorder, for three and a half years, and after numerous drug therapies and treatments, it was decided that this was the last and only hope. Through the bone marrow registry, an unrelated perfect match had been found for her. This hospital in Seattle was *the first* and *the best* hospital for unrelated bone marrow transplants in the whole country. As Becky wrote in her Christmas letter that year, "I've been led here by God to receive a chance at renewed life." My parents and Becky had traveled to Seattle from St. Louis by car so that she could receive her perfect healing. How could this have happened?

I thought back to the last two conversations I had with Becky. I had flown out to Seattle for Christmas and spent hours and hours in the hospital, sitting next to her bed. She had to be behind a clear plastic barrier so she would be protected from any germs or infections because the chemotherapy made her immune system so dangerously low. She laughed at me while I tried and failed miserably to put on the gown, booties, mask, hair thing, and gloves, and then would have to start all over again when I had to blow my nose. While I was still in Seattle, she was moved into a different room where she was not behind the barrier. It was the day I was leaving, so I went to her room to say good-bye before I went to the airport. During the time I was in Seattle, I had developed a slight cold, so had to wear a mask around the floor she was on. I remember standing at the foot of her bed, touching her toes, and saying good-bye. She beckoned me to her side for a hug, and I tearfully said, "I can't, Beck. I love you." I did not realize at the time that this would be the last time I would see my sister.

Back at home in Chicago that next week, I called Becky at the hospital. The news was wonderful! The transplant was a success in that her blood counts were sky high and she was even walking around her floor a bit. We chatted like sisters do about what was next. Being the hard-working perfectionist that she was, she was anxious to "get back to work" on life, which at that time included finishing her second college degree in Lutheran secondary education, planning her wedding to her fiancé, Greg, and maybe even writing a book about her experiences at the hospital so others could benefit from her challenges. For example, before she lost her hair, she had us take pictures of her with long hair, then the short haircut she had done to celebrate the transplant, and then the bald head. She was an avid scrapbooker! Anyway, after talking on the phone for at least an hour, I knew she was tired and needed her rest, so I grudgingly but happily told her I loved her and said good-bye. It was a joyful sister chat that was also our last on this earth. Why, God, why?

During all the difficulties of Becky's illness, we received hundreds and hundreds of cards from Christians all over the country. The amazing thing was that my parents and Becky both received the same Bible passage over and over: Jeremiah 29:11 NIV, which says, " 'For I know the plans I have for you,' declares the LORD, 'plans to prosper you and not to harm you, plans to give you hope and a future.' " Wow! Becky and my parents were given such comfort, hope, and motivation for joyful living through these words of God. You would never have known or even guessed that my sister was sick by the way that she lived her busy life.

Becky loved life and loved her Lord. As always happens at visitations and funerals, we heard many stories of how Becky had touched the lives of others.

While in high school, Becky was state champion gymnast, cheerleader, and ranked third in her senior class. Numerous team members, coaches, teachers, and classmates traveled from Indiana for the funeral. Her high school actually had put on a benefit dinner for her that ironically took place on the day she died. Her geometry teacher spoke after the funeral of how Becky had witnessed to him while she was in college, as he shared difficulties he was having with his teenage son. Her fiancé's roommate also spoke of how Becky witnessed to him through her words and actions of Christ's love, and how he is today a Christian. A sorority sister from college, named Heather, told of how Becky stayed up all night with her after she went through a painful break-up, knowing that Heather might be suicidal. Heather is today a doctor, having done her thesis on aplastic anemia, using Becky's records as a case study.

How did God expect me to get through this loss? Becky was fifteen months younger than me, my best friend from birth. We shared everything from gymnastics, dance, the circus, bunk beds, clothes, talks about anything and everything important to us. I've heard of how twins sometimes have their own language that only they understand. Becky and I had a language and a look that we would share with each other that would just make the other one crack up until our sides hurt. She was an amazing person, scholar, friend, and Christian who wanted to share her faith and knowledge with teenagers as a Lutheran high school teacher. I was devastated and numb, and many times I had a hard time getting out of bed and facing my class of fourth graders at the Lutheran school where I was teaching. How could I share the love of Jesus with them when I felt so empty inside? Thankfully, as Becky wrote in her Christmas letter before she died, "I've learned that even when you don't have the strength to pray, someone else always will." I think my fourth graders prayed like you could not believe that God would take away my sadness, and that I'd remember that Becky was in heaven with Jesus. My students, their families, my church, my school, my family, and my friends sustained me with those prayers that I wasn't ready to pray yet. Day by day, as I taught religion class, I heard my school kids give the answers to questions that I knew but needed to hear. Bible study, church every Sunday—even the day after we got that terrible phone call, when I was so weak from exhaustion and grief that Joel and our friends literally helped me to stand—because in God's house I found comfort in His Word.

In the Bible I turned again to the powerful words of Jeremiah 29:11: " 'For I know the plans I have for you,' declares the LORD, 'plans to prosper you and not to harm you, plans to give you hope and a future.' " The words were so powerful, in fact, that I wanted to be angry with God because I felt betrayed. Yet, in the throes of overwhelming grief, my heavenly Father showed me that Becky had prospered, was not harmed, and was given the ultimate hope and future. She had that perfect healing we all hope and pray for—life in heaven. No more blood transfusions, bone marrow aspirations, chemotherapy, sickness, sadness, or disappointment. Only joy!

Today, ten years later, I can tell you that it still saddens me that my parents lost a daughter, my brother and I lost a sister, Greg lost a future wife, and my children never knew their aunt. But Jesus came, died, and rose for Becky and for all of us so that we could live with Him forever. It's hard to be angry with God knowing that His plans for us to prosper are eternal plans.

Growth through testing! As you reflect on the trials in your life, ask God for insight from His Word to help you deal with the trials, learn from His presence with you in their midst, and prepare you for testing that lies ahead. In the process, God's Spirit can make you sensitive to the needs of others facing similar trials and help you lift them up with the comfort of Christ. When we have no answers to the "why" questions, God points us to the suffering and death of His Son, Jesus, on our behalf. "He Himself bore our sins in His body on the tree, that we might die to sin and live to righteousness. By His wounds you have been healed" (1 Peter 2:24). God's heart beats steadily with our hearts, especially in times of testing.

Experiencing Word-Transformed Lives

And we, who with unveiled faces all reflect
the Lord's glory, are being transformed into
His likeness with ever-increasing glory,
which comes from the Lord, who is the Spirit.
(2 Corinthians 3:18 NIV)

NIV 2011: And we all, who with unveiled
faces contemplate the Lord's glory, are being
transformed into His image with ever-
increasing glory, which comes from the Lord,
who is the Spirit.

ESV: And we all, with unveiled face, beholding
the glory of the Lord, are being transformed
into the same image from one degree of glory
to another. For this comes from the Lord who
is the Spirit.

The Word of Christ transforms lives all of the time across generations and cultures. Meeting and studying the Word with transformed people fills me with joy, strengthens my faith, and deepens my confidence in the power and relevance of God's Word. In earlier chapters, I described our LifeLight community, which takes me deep into the Word each week and connects that Word with their lives and mine. God is bringing real growth in each person and in our group through serious study, honest sharing, and genuine caring.

The individual stories of people such as Dr. Alvin Mueller, Minnie Krieg, the Rabers, Pavel Uhorskai, and Dr. Oswald Hoffmann witness to lives transformed by the Holy Spirit, saints and sinners all, reflecting the Lord's glory.

Consider influential people in your life who have encouraged you in your Christian faith. What drew you to them? In what ways did you see Christ reflected in their lives? How did God's Word transform their lives?

Paul writes to the Corinthian Christians about how the new covenant of God's grace through Jesus Christ is filling them with the glory of the Lord. Their purpose in life as believers is to let the light of Christ radiate from their face to others as the Spirit of the Lord transforms them (2 Corinthians 3:18). Paul brings the apostolic Word to them, not distorting it in any way but "by the open statement of the truth" (2 Corinthians 4:2). He adds, "For what we proclaim is not ourselves, but Jesus Christ as Lord, with ourselves as your servants for Jesus' sake. For God, who said, 'Let light shine out of darkness,' has shone in our hearts to give the light of the knowledge of the glory of God in the face of Christ" (2 Corinthians 4:5–6). The Word of Christ transforms lives!

Consider how the Word of the Lord transformed the prophet Jeremiah at an early age and continued that transforming process throughout his difficult ministry in turbulent times. How might God's Word be transforming your life as you live out your daily calling?

JEREMIAH'S CALL: THE WORD OF THE LORD

The word of the LORD came to me, saying.
(Jeremiah 1:4)

What is God calling you to do with your life? How can you best serve Him? How do you know whether you are responding to your own desires or to His purposes for your life? These questions challenge every Christian. While Jeremiah, as an Old Testament prophet, received God's call directly from Him, and New Testament ministers of the Word receive their call through the Church, we will seek guidelines in Jeremiah for every Christian's calling.

Living in a definite historical setting, "in the days of Josiah the son of Amon, king of Judah, in the thirteenth year of his reign" (verse 2), "Jeremiah, the son of Hilkiah, one of the priests who were in Anathoth" (verse 1), received a definite call from God. Not Jeremiah's personal whims, not a carefully worked out vocational plan with the help of guidance counselors, not a radical vision of his own making, but the clear, simple, direct Word of the Lord. That Word provided both the direction and the power to answer God's call. Ultimately, the Word of the Lord was made flesh and dwelt among us, full of grace and truth: namely, Jesus, the crucified and risen Savior.

In our specific historical situation, with our own personal background, we turn not to our own whims or to a carefully contrived plan for reaching the top of the corporate ladder or to frenetic visions for overcoming midlife crisis. We simply seek the Word of the Lord speaking to our heart. In that Word, received corporately among God's people and individually in our solitude, we find both direction for daily service and power flowing from the cross of our

Lord Jesus Christ, the Word made flesh. Yes, Jeremiah's call and ours begin with the Word of the Lord.

JEREMIAH'S CALL: SET APART AS PROPHET

Before I formed you in the womb I knew you,
and before you were born I consecrated you;
I appointed you as a prophet to the nations.
(Jeremiah 1:5)

We listen to the Word of the Lord, addressed to us for our lives. What do we hear? God's Word to Jeremiah issues a jarring call: he is set apart as a prophet to the nations. "Before I formed you in the womb I knew you, and before you were born I consecrated you; I appointed you as a prophet to the nations."

Jeremiah lived in a troubled time. Judah was in much turmoil, with mighty nations seeking to control and destroy her; there was much wickedness within Judah, including idolatry, injustice, and reliance on political manipulation rather than on God. Jeremiah a prophet of God in such a time? A prophet to Judah? Overwhelming. A prophet to the nations? Impossible. Yet the Word of the Lord clearly tells him of his call to be a prophet. God reveals that he has been set apart for this role even before he was born. He has been appointed and prepared all his life for this prophetic ministry. What a call indeed!

What about your call? Not exactly like Jeremiah's. Different historical situation. Different person. Different calling. Yet before God formed you in the womb, He knew you. He knew you with His tender love as Creator and with His forgiving love as Redeemer. Christ's death and resurrection avails for you. Before you were born, He set you apart. That's what *holy* means: set apart for God's purposes. Baptized in the triune God, you have been set apart through water and the Word. He has called you to make your bold confession of Jesus as your Savior, to give an account for the hope you have because of Him! What a call, indeed!

JEREMIAH'S CALL:
DOUBTS EXPRESSED

Then I said, "Ah, Lord GOD! Behold, I do not know how to speak for I am only a youth." (Jeremiah 1:6)

The Word of the Lord speaks. We hear. "Consecrated you . . . a prophet to the nations" (verse 5). A tremendous challenge for Jeremiah. A difficult application for us as modern-day proclaimers of Christ's love. We hear. But now what?

Jeremiah expresses serious doubts about his own ability to answer God's call. He responds, "Ah Lord GOD! . . . I do not know how to speak for I am only a youth." He trembles. What good is a prophet who can't speak? Echoes of Moses by the burning bush! How can an immature teenager (which Jeremiah may have been) stand before kings and princes? Good questions. Serious doubts. Jeremiah would indeed be tested beyond human endurance—physically, emotionally, and spiritually. He would suffer rejection after rejection. Assurance and maturity would come from God's words and His steady presence. For the moment, though, Jeremiah's doubts remain.

Do you have serious doubts about your ability to speak God's Word and stand boldly as a Christian in difficult situations? Do you feel like a child in your spiritual maturity even though you may have gray hair and a solid standing in society? Like Jeremiah, we can also expect stiff tests of our faith as we answer God's call to service—possible rejections, day-by-day temptations, and flagging zeal. "Ah Lord GOD! . . . I do not know how to speak for I am only a youth."

We have serious doubts, but God will supply the words to speak as well as His forgiving presence in Jesus Christ, the Crucified, to mature us. The call stands.

JEREMIAH'S CALL: GOD'S ASSURANCE

Do not be afraid of them, for I am with you to deliver you, declares the LORD. (Jeremiah 1:8)

Jeremiah has real doubts about his ability to serve as a prophet to the nations. He hears the call and knows that God speaks. Afraid and uncertain, he needs reassurance. The Lord declares, "Do not be afraid of them, for I am with you to deliver you." Words of promise and comfort. Jeremiah takes the assignment and begins to speak God's Word of judgment and mercy. How he will need those words of assurance as he repeatedly faces kings and priests with a message of repentance! They plot against his life. They arrest and imprison him. They beat him and leave him to die in an open cistern. He wants to die. He complains against God. Nevertheless, he keeps speaking the Word of the Lord, and always there are those words of assurance for him: "Do not be afraid of them, for I am with you to deliver you."

We need those words also. We hear God's call and know that He speaks to us. We also see the world in which we live—immorality, cheating, scoffing at religions, power plays, and social climbing. Real doubts grip our hearts when we try to proclaim the Word of the Lord to our age. The Lord declares, "Do not be afraid of them, for I am with you to deliver you." We see the Lord come into a world that rejects Him. We hear the taunts and feel the whip gouge His back. We observe His faithfulness on the cross and hear His loving Word of forgiveness. We experience His forgiveness in our lives and dwell on His continuing Word of comfort. We falter. We speak hesitatingly. We wince at rejection. But we keep speaking His message, for those words of assurance continue, "Do not be afraid of them, for I am with you to deliver you."

JEREMIAH'S CALL: GOD'S WORDS IN MY MOUTH

> Then the LORD put out His hand and touched my mouth. And the LORD said to me, "Behold, I have put My words in your mouth." (Jeremiah 1:9)

The Word of the Lord came to Jeremiah, announcing his call. He learned that he was set apart as a prophet to the nations. Doubts rose within him that he could not speak and was only a child. God's assurance came with the words, "Do not be afraid of them" (verse 8). Now the Lord provides Jeremiah with the words he will speak as a prophet. "Then the LORD put out His hand and touched my mouth. And the LORD said to me, 'Behold, I have put My words in your mouth.' "

That Word consumes Jeremiah. He later writes, "His word is in my heart like a fire, a fire shut up in my bones. I am weary of holding it in; indeed, I cannot" (Jeremiah 20:9). He simply obeys God and speaks powerfully against Judah's sins. Sometimes he illustrates the Word with symbols of God's message, but always he communicates God's message. The result—God's Word of judgment is vindicated in the destruction of Jerusalem, and His Word of promise materializes in the new covenant ushered in by Jesus Christ, the Crucified One.

What a powerful description of God's call! He specially entrusted Jeremiah with His very own words of judgment and mercy. He also gives His Word to called and ordained servants as they publicly preach the Word and administer the Sacraments. They are to speak God's Word, not their own message. He also touches the mouth of each Christian and puts in His words. We are touched by the Word in Baptism and made new creatures in Christ. We feed on that Word as it is proclaimed by pastors. We share that Word with others in our daily calling. Yes, Jeremiah's call has much to teach us about God's call in our lives. God's Word holds the answers.

Clearly, God's Word transformed Jeremiah! God's Word has also transformed you in your Baptism. You can live more deeply in the Word of Christ by joining other believers in an ongoing study of God's Word as you live together with unveiled faces so that others will see Christ the Savior in your face and your life.

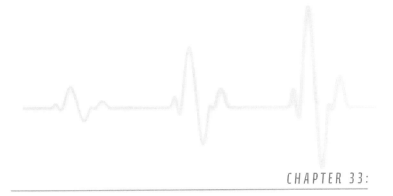

Building a Biblical Worldview

The secret things belong to the Lord our God,
but the things that are revealed belong to us
and to our children forever, that we may do all
the words of this law. (Deuteronomy 29:29)

We began *Heartbeat!* with a series of questions: Would you like to discover the secret of how to live with passion for Christ in your personal life, your family, your neighborhood, your church, your community, your place of work, and your world? Would you like to live for Christ not only in the moment of each day's challenges and opportunities but also with consistency over a lifetime of hills and valleys?

These questions are personal and palpable, calling for practical answers. The culture that envelopes us demands quick and easy answers. Perhaps you have felt impatient for those practical answers as you have been reading this book. The stories of people with passion for Christ are great, but how do they interact with my story? Yes, I do experience passions that drain and passions that lead to bondage, but how do I overcome them each day in my burdensome, pressurized little world? David confessed his terrible sins and received forgiveness, but how do I keep receiving God's forgiveness on the treadmill of my sinful life? I believe in God's Word and want to make new discoveries that will help me live joyfully and freely; why do the many words surrounding me from radio, television, and the Internet drown out the few words from God that stick in my head and heart? I want to live deeply in the Word of Christ for comfort, strength, and guidance, yet my limited time and fuzzy focus on God's Word prevent me from going deeper.

I appreciate your honesty and your frustration. If your spiritual heartbeat depended on your efforts, all would be lost. If today's culture was justified in demanding formula solutions and quick, easy answers, you would be in serious trouble. However, the culture is absolutely wrong, and your spiritual heart beats by God's grace for Christ's sake through faith. You are baptized into Christ! Your very questions reveal God's Spirit working through the Word of Christ.

The final reason for living deeply in the Word of Christ is building a biblical worldview. Living counter culture and against the opposition of your sinful flesh, you are shaped by the Word to understand the world as God sees it.

Israel stands ready to cross the Jordan River and to conquer the Promised Land after forty painful years in the wilderness. Their hearts are filled with fear at the thought of a river in spring flood stage and giant enemies in the land. God's revealed covenant grace at Sinai, including the giving of the majestic Ten Commandments to Moses, seems far removed from their current practical plight. They even face a change in leadership from Moses to Joshua. Sound familiar?

Moses takes them deeper into God's Word because they need that Word both short-term and for the long haul. *Deuteronomy* literally means "the second giving of the Law." Moses tells them that they were there with their forefathers at the holy mountain. His covenant there is His covenant with this new generation. They are His chosen people by virtue of His mighty acts in Egypt and at the Red Sea. He will bless them as they put their trust in His salvation. He will supply them with all they need to cross the Jordan and conquer the land He is giving them as an inheritance. Through them, God will raise up One who will save them and the world from sin once for all.

By His grace, they must live counter culture against the idolatry and immoral lifestyle of the people in the land. They must renounce self-help and the desires of their sinful flesh, which caused the bodies of their rebellious forefathers to litter the wilderness. In short, to counter the sinful worldview of the surrounding nations, they need a biblical worldview, which only God can reveal. Moses speaks:

> The secret things belong to the LORD our God, but the things that are revealed belong to us and to our children forever, that we may do all the words of this law. (Deuteronomy 29:29)

God reveals everything needed for salvation and a daily life of obedience. Each generation builds a biblical worldview that enables it to live counter culture as His people and therefore find practical answers for each day and for the long term. Scripture is not the human record of what ancient peoples believed about God. Scripture is God's revelation about His love and His saving plan for the universe from eternity to eternity after Christ's second coming. We will never know all the secret things of God, but He has revealed Himself to us as His people and through us to the world. In the introduction, entitled "God's Secret Revealed," we quoted the apostle Paul, living with passion in the Word of Christ:

> I became a minister according to the stewardship

> from God that was given to me for you, to make the word of God fully known, the mystery hidden for ages and generations but now revealed to His saints. To them God chose to make known how great among the Gentiles are the riches of the glory of this mystery, which is Christ in you, the hope of glory. (Colossians 1:25–27)

We build a biblical worldview as we carefully study all of Scripture, Old Testament and New Testament, over our lifetime. When we are open to God's Spirit leading us, we learn about God's plan and how it unfolded through each generation. We observe how His grace works through sinful human beings to bring His salvation in the Messiah. We learn from biblical history about spiritual warfare, God's judgment against human rebellion and sin, God's mercy and promises fulfilled, the centrality of Christ's incarnation, ministry, obedient suffering and death, glorious resurrection and ascension, and the establishment of the Church after Pentecost with a worldwide mission until Christ comes again.

The biblical worldview takes on fresh meaning as we face today's world with its specific challenges. Our immersion in Scripture and its worldview helps us better understand local, national, and world events and how our personal issues interact with God's world. We realize that the world does not revolve around us but rather around God. We live by His grace and forgiveness as part of His people, on behalf of the world, in view of eternity.

Here is one example of how God's people at one point in their history responded to a biblical worldview with action from their heart, God's heartbeat. Consider how you might apply this story to your own story.

BUILDING WITH THE HEART

So we rebuilt the wall till all of it reached half its height, for the people worked with all their heart. (Nehemiah 4:6 NIV)

What a task! Rebuilding the walls of Jerusalem. The city lies in shambles. After years of captivity in Babylon, a small group returns to the scene of former glory. Where to begin? Led by Nehemiah, the people begin to rebuild the city walls. Opposition mounts. Nearby people threaten to attack every day. The Jews have to build with a sword in one hand and a trowel in the other. What obstacles!

Nevertheless, the walls are built because the people work with all their heart. Previously, Judah's heart strayed from God to idolatry and personal gain. Now, repentant and chastened by captivity, the returning exiles desire with all their heart to restore the sacred city as a monument of praise to God. They are willing to struggle and sacrifice to accomplish the task.

Whether brick or mortar are involved, we face challenges in our daily lives at home, church, our place of work or in our community to which the imagery of building may apply. We live out our God-given vocations aware of the difficulties. What a task! Money seems lacking and relationships often lie in shambles with much brokenness, misunderstanding, hurt, and jealousy. Opposition mounts as other people say it can't be done. What obstacles!

We can build when we work together with all our heart. When our hearts stray from God, we get wrapped up in selfish desires and seek material gain. God shatters our self-serving dreams and points us to His heart, a heart willingly broken on the cross in payment for our sins. Chastened, repentant, forgiven, and restored, we begin to build. God gives us a heart for the work. The building proceeds to the glory of God. God's kingdom comes. His Church is built into a temple of living stones. What a joy to participate with all our heart!

GOD'S BUILDING PROJECT

So the wall was completed . . . in fifty-two days. . . . They realized that this work had been done with the help of our God. (Nehemiah 6:15–16b NIV)

Building project complete! The walls were rebuilt in fifty-two days: a major accomplishment. Despite the constant opposition, Nehemiah completes the city walls. Yes, the people build with all their heart. Yes, Nehemiah is a capable leader. However, something far more significant leads to this amazing result.

God is the builder! He wants those walls completed. He wants the faithful remnant to praise Him again in Jerusalem. God's people know who deserves credit. They assemble to hear Ezra read the Law from daybreak to noon (Nehemiah 8:2–3). They then thank and praise God in celebration with Nehemiah's reminder: "The joy of the LORD is your strength" (verse 10c NIV). Even the enemies of the Jews must recognize the rebuilt city walls as God's building project. We are told they "[lose] their self-confidence, because they realized that this work had been done with the help of our God."

When we participate in the physical building of a church or Christian school, we certainly rejoice when the project is complete. When we see a Christian fellowship growing in size, depth, and closeness, we feel a sense of accomplishment. Yes, people work together with all their heart. Yes, faithful pastors and lay members provide good leadership. However, something far more significant is involved.

God is the builder! He wants His Church to grow and serve Him. He built His Church on the foundation of the apostles and prophets, with Jesus Christ as the chief cornerstone. Christ gave His life for the Church. We assemble to hear His life-changing Word and to celebrate God's grace in sacramental worship. Even enemies of the Gospel have to recognize that "this work [has] been done with the help of our God."

I hope that God has filled your heart with excitement to continue building a biblical worldview. I pray that as God has revealed the hope of Christ in you, the hope of glory, you are encouraged as you seek answers to your daily questions regarding passionate living for Christ.

We now move to the final part of *Heartbeat!*, "Living God's Passion for the World." I pray that we approach this revelation of God with the humility of Paul's doxology in Romans 11:

> Oh, the depth of the riches and wisdom and knowledge of God! How unsearchable are His judgments and how inscrutable His ways!
>
> "For who has known the mind of the Lord, or who has been His counselor?"
>
> "Or who has given a gift to Him that He might be repaid?"
>
> For from Him and through Him and to Him are all things. To Him be glory forever. Amen. (Romans 11:33–36)

PART SIX

LIVING GOD'S
PASSION FOR THE WORLD

> I will give you a new heart, and a new spirit
> I will put within you. And I will remove the
> heart of stone from your flesh and give you a
> heart of flesh. And I will put my Spirit within
> you, and cause you to walk in my statutes and
> be careful to obey my rules. (Ezekiel 36:26–27)

You may have started reading this *Heartbeat!* book with a wrong
understanding of living with passion for Christ, thinking that
you needed to create that passion within yourself. If so, you
would be discouraged on any given day when you feel drained
and demotivated. Or you might experience that passion for
Christ occasionally but realize that you cannot sustain it for a
long period of time.

I hope that you have come to understand that only God's passion for the world can fill you with passion for Christ daily and for
your entire life. For that to happen, you have needed a heart transplant. The word of the Lord came to the prophet Ezekiel with this
message for the house of Israel:

> I will sprinkle clean water on you, and you shall be
> clean from all your uncleannesses, and from all your
> idols I will cleanse you. And I will give you a new
> heart, and a new spirit I will put within you. And I
> will remove the heart of stone from your flesh and
> give you a heart of flesh. (Ezekiel 36:25–26)

Stubborn and rebellious, Israel had failed to live with passion for God and had turned to idols. Now a gracious God cleanses them with water and replaces their stony hearts with a responsive, trusting, obedient heart of flesh. God adds, "I will put My Spirit within you, and cause you to walk in My statutes and be careful to obey My rules" (Ezekiel 36:27)

Alive with the heartbeat of the Reformation—justified by God's grace for Christ's sake through faith—we have received a heart transplant in our Baptism. By daily confession and absolution, God's Spirit uses the Word of Christ to supply God's steady heart-beat—His will that we are united with Him—each new day and throughout our life. In that way, we joyfully live God's passion for the world. This final part of *Heartbeat!* helps us grasp God's passion for the world, grow as a planting of the Lord, and live God's passion for creation, against injustice and idolatry, for salvation through Jesus, and for reaching all nations through the Church.

CHAPTER 34:

Grasping God's Passion for the World

That Christ may dwell in your hearts through faith—that you, being rooted and grounded in love, may have strength to comprehend with all the saints what is the breadth and length and height and depth, and to know the love of Christ that surpasses knowledge, that you may be filled with all the fullness of God. (Ephesians 3:17–19)

I have known this passage from Paul's Letter to the Ephesians at least since my teenage years, and I have never been able to get my arms around it. I studied Ephesians in seminary under an outstanding biblical scholar. I still could not begin to comprehend its meaning. After a lifetime of pastoral ministry, life experience, and extensive Bible study, I still stand in awe of Paul's prayer. I do understand, however, that it describes God's passion for the world.

Indeed, passion does not start with me. It begins with God. How can I live God's passion for the world if I do not yet understand it? At the very least, I have daily reason to be shaped by the Word of Christ. I have daily reason to fall on my knees in praise and adoration. I have daily reason to confess my feeble efforts to understand and grasp. I have daily reason to thank God for answering part of Paul's prayer "that according to the riches of His glory He may grant you to be strengthened with power through His Spirit in your inner being, so that Christ may dwell in your hearts through faith" (Ephesians 3:16–17a). "Jesus loves me! This I know, For the Bible tells me so" (*LSB* 588:1). I can at least confess my tunnel vision.

TUNNEL VISION TRANSFORMED

As Your name, O God, so Your praise reaches to the ends of the earth. (Psalm 48:10)

Some people suffer from an eye problem called tunnel vision. The eyes can only see straight ahead with no peripheral vision at all. So much of God's creation goes unseen. One cannot drive a car safely or participate successfully in athletics unless one has "tunnel vision" while doing so. With a world to see, reality lies only straight ahead.

Unfortunately, Christians often view God's Church and the Christian life through tunnel vision. Reality is limited to my home, my work, and my congregation. I see no one else. I fail to see other Christians, other countries, other peoples in need of the Gospel. I insist that God operates only within my field of vision.

The psalmist widens our vision tremendously by speaking of "the ends of the earth." Israel often suffered from tunnel vision. Jonah suffered God's wrath by refusing to preach to Nineveh and trying to run in the opposite direction, but God's name and His praise reach "to the ends of the earth." He made the world. He sent His Son to die for the world. He spreads His Gospel Word over all nations.

My tunnel vision broadens considerably when I hear about a wonderful Savior from the Japanese Lutheran Hour speaker, work with fellow Lutherans from South Africa and Tanzania, talk to enthusiastic Haitian students, or learn of exciting Christian fellowship groups in Communist China. Indeed, God has made me a world Christian and transformed my tunnel vision into eyes that see a universe alive with His name and His praise.

Confessing tunnel vision, we can let God open our eyes little by little over a lifetime so that we grasp more and more God's love and concern for the world. We discover that love in a sunrise or a snowflake, a bright red cardinal at the birdfeeder or a wild turkey in the woods. We see His concern for the world in a four-year-old child sitting silently on the lap of a recent widower, helping him cry. He reaches out in the hymn verse sung at the bedside of a dying friend or father and a Bible verse sent by e-mail or texting at just the right time.

We do need to know as much about God's passion for the world as we can. Regular and deeper study of His Word will open up many new understandings as the Spirit works both subtly and powerfully. Study with others will unlock fresh insights into God's passion for the world. Every day, He demonstrates His passion in the nitty-gritty events of our lives. However, knowledge alone falls short. Paul describes God's passion as "the love that surpasses knowledge" (Ephesians 3:19). That's why living with passion in the Word of Christ never grows old, and the *Heartbeat!* adventure continues as long as our physical heart beats as well as throughout eternity in God's presence before the throne and the Lamb.

Actually living God's passion for the world increases day by day our grasp of the dimensions of His love through Christ. Read the stories of His love. Tell the stories of His love. Live the story of His love.

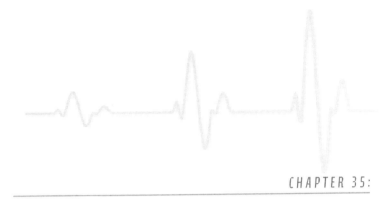

Growing as
"A Planting of the Lord"

They will be called oaks of righteousness, a
planting of the LORD for the display of His
splendor. (Isaiah 61:3c NIV)

Would you like to discover the secret of how to live with passion
for Christ? This opening question of *Heartbeat!* found an answer
in Paul's words, "Christ in you, the hope of glory" (Colossians
1:27). Only God can reveal His secret (mystery) through His
Word and that secret is always Christ as the fulfillment of God's
plan of salvation through the ages for all people, Jew and Gentile
alike. It is an "open" secret for those who believe. And Christ
dwells in them through their baptismal faith, the sure hope of
glory. Scripture unlocks this powerful secret in many places with
the imagery of God's garden planted to produce fruit. Living
God's passion for the world, which can scarcely be grasped by
our puny minds and hearts, begins with the basic insight that
we are growing as a planting of the Lord. Let this rich scriptural
imagery speak for itself.

Isaiah presents the coming Messiah speaking to Zion, God's
Old Testament remnant, and to the New Testament Church about
His saving mission:

The Spirit of the Sovereign LORD is on me, because the LORD has anointed me to preach good news to the poor. He has sent me to bind up the brokenhearted, to proclaim freedom for the captives and release from darkness for the prisoners, to proclaim the year of the LORD's favor and the day of vengeance of our God, to comfort all who mourn, and provide for those who grieve in Zion—to bestow on them a crown of beauty instead of ashes, the oil of gladness instead of mourning, and a garment of praise instead of a spirit of despair. They will be called oaks of righteousness, a planting of the LORD for the display of His splendor. (Isaiah 61:1–3 NIV)

Jesus of Nazareth, fresh from His Baptism and wilderness temptation, applies these words of Isaiah to Himself in His home-town synagogue (Luke 4:14–21). This Good News includes Christ's death and resurrection *for* the world and His dwelling *in* believers, clothed in His righteousness ("a garment of praise," Isaiah 61:3 NIV). The powerful imagery, "They will be called oaks of righteousness, a planting of the LORD for the display of His splendor" (verse 3c NIV), is nothing less than God's secret revealed: "Christ in you, the hope of glory" (Colossians 1:27). The Church grows as a planting of the Lord and displays Christ's splendor to the world. You are oaks of righteousness by God's grace.

John's Gospel further connects disciples to "Christ in you, the hope of glory" by using vineyard imagery as "a planting of the LORD." Jesus teaches:

I am the true vine, and My Father is the vinedresser. Every branch in Me that does not bear fruit He takes away, and every branch that does bear fruit He prunes, that it may bear more fruit. Already you are clean because of the word that I have spoken to you. Abide in Me, and I in you. As the branch cannot bear fruit by itself, unless it abides in the vine, neither can you, unless you abide in Me. I am the vine; you are the branches. Whoever abides in Me and I in him, he it is that bears much fruit, for apart from Me you can do nothing. If anyone does not abide in Me he is thrown away like a branch and withers; and the branches are gathered, thrown into the fire, and burned. If you abide in Me, and My words abide in you, ask whatever you wish, and it will be done for you. By this My Father is glorified, that you bear much fruit and so prove to be My disciples. (John 15:1–8)

These simple, powerful words capture the essence of this entire book, "Living with Passion *in* the Word of Christ" (emphasis added). On that basis, we separate ourselves from worldly passions that drain and lead to bondage as we live counter culture. On that basis, we discover the Word of Christ in constantly new ways and live deeply in God's Word as we crave spiritual milk, eat a steady diet of solid food, and embrace Christ-help. Suddenly, other Scripture passages open up to our understanding. For examples, we view the contrast in Psalm 1 between the blessed and the wicked. The blessed person "walks not in the counsel of the wicked, nor stands in the way of sinners, nor sits in the seat of scoffers; but his delight is in the law of the LORD, and on His law he meditates day and night" (Psalm 1:1–2). Now drink into your soul the "planting of the Lord" imagery:

He is like a tree planted by streams of water that yields its fruit in its season, and its leaf does not wither. In all that he does, he prospers. (Psalm 1:3)

Further, absorb into your heart these words from Psalm 92:

> The righteous flourish like the palm tree and grow
> like a cedar in Lebanon. They are planted in the
> house of the LORD; they flourish in the courts of our
> God. They still bear fruit in old age; they are ever full
> of sap and green, to declare that the LORD is upright;
> He is my rock, and there is no unrighteousness in
> Him. (Psalm 92:12–15)

How consistent is this biblical imagery! We are, as part of God's Church on earth, "a planting of the LORD for the display of His splendor" (Isaiah 61:3c NIV). Remaining in Christ, the true vine, and His saving Word, we declare His righteousness to the world so that lives are transformed by the Spirit's power. Isaiah further describes how God strengthens and sustains us as "a planting of the LORD" in a wicked world:

> The LORD will guide you always; He will satisfy your
> needs in a sun-scorched land and will strengthen
> your frame. You will be like a well-watered garden,
> like a spring whose waters never fail. (Isaiah 58:11
> NIV)

No wonder, then, that Paul does not describe our walk by the Spirit as the works of the Spirit fighting the works of the flesh. Rather, he contrasts the works of the flesh—"sexual immorality, impurity, sensuality, idolatry," and so on (Galatians 5:19–21)—with the *fruit* of the Spirit: "love, joy, peace, patience, kindness, goodness, faithfulness, gentleness, self-control" (Galatians 5:22–23). We are, after all, "a planting of the LORD for the display of His splendor" (Isaiah 61:3c NIV). Jesus says to His disciples not long before His journey to the cross:

> You did not choose Me, but I chose you and appointed

you that you should go and bear fruit and that your
fruit should abide. (John 15:16)

The biblical imagery in this chapter challenges the soul of today's culture and perhaps your own lifestyle. Our culture shouts, "Do, do, do! Strive, claw, fight! Set goals, be productive, measure results! Save time, fill your days, maximize your online searches and conferences, your smartphone usage, and your instant responses! Climb the ladder by relentless networking!" And God does provide modern technology, sensible business practices, and effective communication for carrying out our callings.

However, it all begins—our desire to live God's passion for the world—with the biblical imagery of growing as "a planting of the LORD for the display of His splendor."

I write these words at the beginning of spring. Unexpectedly, a heavy wet snowstorm briefly blanketed our tulip tree in bloom and the beautiful magnolias of our neighbor as temperatures plummeted below freezing. Today, the sun shines, the daffodils are blooming, and the redbuds are beginning to open up. The plantings of the Lord all around me burst forth with passion for the display of His splendor. I cannot control that symphony of life, nor do I desire to do so, but I can stand in awe and praise Him for His bounty.

In the same way, I rejoice that He has made you and me, His special people, whose stories I am honored to tell, and His whole Church on earth through the generations. He has made us "a planting of the LORD for the display of His splendor." I pray that I might bloom where I am planted. We are better prepared to let God's Spirit reveal what it means to live God's passion for the world, starting with creation.

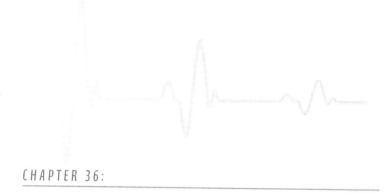

Living God's Passion for Creation

> In the beginning, God created the heavens and the earth. . . . And God said, "Let there be light," and there was light. . . . And God saw everything that He had made, and behold, it was very good. (Genesis 1:1, 3, 31)

> Then the Lord God formed the man of dust from the ground and breathed into his nostrils the breath of life, and the man became a living creature. And the Lord God planted a garden in Eden, in the east, and there He put the man whom He had formed. (Genesis 2:7–8)

God's passion for creation explodes on the first pages of Scripture. He creates out of nothing. He simply speaks the words, and creation happens. By His perfect standards, everything He made is very good. What's more, God personally reaches down to form Adam from the dust of the ground, breathing into his nostrils the breath of life so that Adam becomes a living creature. That's passion!

Then God gives Adam and Eve responsibility as the crown of creation to care for the whole creation:

Be fruitful and multiply and fill the earth and subdue it and have dominion over the fish of the sea and over the birds of the heavens and over every living thing that moves on the earth. (Genesis 1:28–29)

God's passion for creation was passed on to the first human creatures and to us. Adam and Eve's disobedience (eating the forbidden fruit of the tree of the knowledge of good and evil, Genesis 3:1–7) and rebellion (desiring to be like God) led to separation from God and disharmony in creation. Nevertheless, God's passion for creation, including human beings, continues in His promise of protection, provision, and a Messiah to usher in a new creation through His death on a cross, the gift of faith, and a new people of God, the Church (2 Corinthians 5:14–21).

Therefore, if anyone is in Christ, he is a new creation. The old has passed away; behold, the new has come. All this is from God, who through Christ reconciled us to Himself and gave us the ministry of reconciliation. (2 Corinthians 5:17–18)

Because of Christ, we live God's love and concern for creation every day.

MY FATHER'S WORLD

And now, Father, glorify Me in Your own presence with the glory that I had with You before the world existed. (John 17:5)

What do you have in common with every person on the face of the globe—red, yellow, black, and white; Asian, African, European, North and South American; Muslim, Hindu, Buddhist, Jew, Christian, and atheist? You live in the Father's world, created by the one true God: Father, Son, and Holy Spirit.

That's what John communicates when he uses the word *world* in John 17:5 to describe the whole universe as God's creation. "In the beginning was the Word, and the Word was with God, and the Word was God. . . . All things were made through Him" (John 1:1, 3). Jesus identifies His role in the creation of His Father's world when He prays in John 17, "And now, Father, glorify Me in Your own presence with the glory that I had with You before the world existed" (verse 5). Then He heads for Calvary to glorify the Father in His death.

As you seek to live God's passion for the world, you can start with a common appreciation of the wonders of creation. Although many people, those with a false religion or no religion at all, will not recognize or understand the Father's world as you do through faith in Jesus the Savior, you live together with them in the same universe as God's created children. Together with them you see the sunrise and sunset, feel the gentle rain, gather the golden grain, fish the streams, and live in families with shelter and daily bread.

When darkness comes, storms rage, famine spreads, and evil destroys, you reach out to bring light, restore calm, provide shelter and food, and help restore order. You also respect the culture, language, and created gifts of others in the Father's world. In turn, you receive thankfully their hospitality and help.

Admitting our own prejudice, divisiveness, and selfishness, we look to Jesus and seek to let His light of salvation shine in the darkness through us.

"MAN AND BEAST YOU SAVE"

Man and beast You save, O LORD. (Psalm 36:6c)

Recently, my wife and I joined a group of Christian friends for a few days for planning, spiritual growth, and recreation. Those days in the mountains provided some delightful views of wildlife. One morning, as I was reading my Bible, I looked out the front window and saw a doe walk right up to the wrought iron fence in front of the patio. She looked straight at me with her ears alert. She sensed no danger and walked in leisurely fashion through the side yard, followed closely by her fawn, and then moved up the mountainside. A few minutes later, her yearling appeared, a little less sure of safety, and with a start, it bounded up the mountainside at a sharper angle. I could not help but think of the psalmist's words, "Man and beast You save, O LORD."

Obviously, these words describe the physical preservation of humans and animals alike in God's creation. In Psalm 50, God speaks to His people about the sacrifices of thanksgiving for His salvation: "For every beast of the forest is Mine, the cattle on a thousand hills" (Psalm 50:10). Then He applies that physical preservation to human beings. "Call upon Me in the day of trouble; I will deliver you, and you shall glorify Me" (Psalm 50:15).

As I watched the doe, I thought of God's salvation through Jesus Christ. The doe went about her daily life, caring for her fawn and releasing her yearling for independent living, just because she knew it was a safe place for her. In the same way, God has brought me into the safe place of God's grace. Despite a cruel and wicked world, despite Satan's attacks, despite my own sinful nature, God sent His Son to bear my punishment on Calvary. Forgiven and set free in Christ through my Baptism, I have been incorporated into God's people, and I enjoy salvation and safety in the arms of my Savior.

From that safe place, I can go about my daily life in family, community, work activities, and the world with thanksgiving to God for physical and spiritual deliverance and with a desire to share that salvation with others: "Man and beast You save, O LORD."

"THE ABUNDANCE OF YOUR HOUSE"

They feast on the abundance of Your house, and You give them drink from the river of Your delights. (Psalm 36:8)

As I reflect on my time in the mountains, the word *abundance* comes to mind: the mountain slopes carpeted in green, the colorful wildflowers, the clear, fast-flowing mountain streams, the picturesque villages of Vail and Beaver Creek, the comfortable mountain home where we stayed, the rich interactions personally and spiritually with our group of friends, and the quiet reading of God's Word in that peaceful setting. This abundance made the words of the psalmist come alive for me. "How precious is Your steadfast love, O God! The children of mankind take refuge in the shadow of Your wings. They feast on the abundance of Your house, and You give them drink from the river of Your delights. For with You is the fountain of life; in Your light do we see light" (Psalm 36:7–9). "Your house" refers to all creation, from which flows the water of life. I thought of the house where we gathered and where we experienced the total blessings of the mountains. What abundance, a gift of God's hand!

Coming from the mountains back to our home on the Mississippi River bluffs of St. Louis, I am moved to share that abundance with others. Jesus says, "I came that they may have life and have it abundantly" (John 10:10). For Him, that meant laying down His life for the sheep as the Good Shepherd. Post-resurrection, Jesus said to His disciples, "As the Father has sent Me, even so I am sending you" (John 20:21). Forgiven, restored, and gifted with abundant life in Christ, we are sent to offer that abundant life to others, living in scarcity and want, physically and spiritually. Abundance of witness to Christ! Hear God's promise by His grace: "Whoever brings blessing will be enriched, and one who waters will himself be watered" (Proverbs 11:25). Reflections from the mountains!

We live God's passion for creation by marveling at the Father's world with all of God's creatures. On a recent South American cruise, we joined other travelers in viewing snow-covered volcanic mountains, rushing cascades, magnificent and colorful glaciers, and clear mountain lakes. Many conversations about our faith in Christ flowed from our passion for God's creation.

However, we also live God's passion for creation when we stand shoulder to shoulder with others to provide acts of mercy at times of natural disasters. God cares for people in need and reaches out through us to rescue them.

HURRICANE KATRINA: THE REALITY

What is man that You are mindful of him, and the son of man that You care for him? (Psalm 8:4)

In the early morning hours of Monday, August 29, 2005, Hurricane Katrina struck the Gulf Coast of Louisiana, Mississippi, and Alabama with winds in excess of 140 miles per hour, causing a destructive sea surge near Gulfport and Biloxi and the eventual flooding of the city of New Orleans. The resultant communication breakdown, collapse of medical facilities, extensive loss of life, gathering of displaced residents under desperate living conditions, and total destruction of commercial and residential property made this killer storm one of the worst natural disasters in U.S. history.

How might the horrible reality of this storm and its effects anchor our faith in the God of our salvation and make us more effective in our witness to Jesus Christ? In Psalm 8, King David reflects on the majesty of God's creation—the heavens, the moon, and the stars in the night sky. He could have included the powerful forces of nature in the wind and the waves. In the face of God's almighty power, he sees how puny human beings are: "What is man that You are mindful of him?" Since we are not the Creator but creatures, and sinful human beings at that, we recognize with David our utter dependence on God's mercy for life and breath and salvation. The reality of Hurricane Katrina demonstrates the total inadequacy of our scientific achievement, our technology, and our national power and wealth. "What is man that You are mindful of him?"

How wonderful that the writer to the Hebrews applies these very verses to Jesus, our Savior: "But we see Him who for a little while was made lower than the angels, namely Jesus, crowned with glory and honor because of the suffering of death, so that by the grace of God He might taste death for everyone" (Hebrews 2:9). A real Savior in death for the ugly reality of Katrina—He is our comfort and our witness!

HURRICANE KATRINA: DOMINION

> You have given him dominion over the works of Your hands; You have put all things under his feet. (Psalm 8:6)

The story of Hurricane Katrina moves far beyond the destructive reality. King David, although fully aware that sinful human beings are puny creatures under the Creator God, recognizes his own stewardship responsibility over the earth: "You have given him dominion over the works of Your hands; You have put all things under his feet." Reflecting with these words God's own words in Genesis, "Let us make man in Our image, after Our likeness. And let them have dominion" (Genesis 1:26), David accepts his leadership role to manage God's affairs on earth.

Before the hurricane, weather forecasters gave scientific warning of the gathering storm and urged evacuation. Local, state, and federal governments tried to respond to the anticipated devastation through advance planning, orderly evacuation, and the placement of personnel and provisions for relief and rescue. They were exercising dominion as stewards. Their stewardship was imperfect due to the ferocity of the storm and unexpected problems. Much blame was directed at their response. Nevertheless, nationwide relief efforts were mounted in the wake of Katrina, involving governmental agencies, the military, not-for-profit organizations such as the Red Cross and church-sponsored relief entities, as well as an international outpouring of money, goods, and services. Human beings were exercising dominion. God worked through these stewardship efforts.

St. Paul applies these verses to Jesus: "And He put all things under His feet and gave Him as head over all things to the church, which is His body" (Ephesians 1:22–23). Confessing the failure of our stewardship efforts as sin, we recognize the dominion of Christ through His death and resurrection. As part of His Church through Baptism, we participate in society to help exercise godly dominion by bringing relief, rescue, and rebuilding after natural disasters such as Katrina. Our humble response ultimately brings witness through the Church to the crucified and risen Savior.

HURRICANE KATRINA: HOPE FOR THE NEEDY

For the needy shall not always be forgotten, and the hope of the poor shall not perish forever. (Psalm 9:18)

Hurricane Katrina placed many people in great need—rich and poor alike, infants and children, senior adults, critically ill patients in evacuated hospitals, people with disabilities, those fleeing and those trapped in the cities, even rescue workers. Lives were threatened and lost. Families were separated. Homes and places of work were destroyed. Many were forced to relocate to other parts of the country. People endured physical illness, mental stress, emotional exhaustion, and spiritual emptiness. Where is hope for the needy?

The psalmist, oppressed by the wicked, sees a God who cares for those in need. He prays, "O Lord, You hear the desire of the afflicted; You will strengthen their heart; You will incline Your ear to do justice to the fatherless and the oppressed" (Psalm 10:17–18). God cares for the physical, mental, emotional, and spiritual needs of His created children.

In the hurricane disaster, God brought hope to the needy through military rescue helicopters, Red Cross emergency shelters, food and bottled water, volunteers, welcoming neighbors in another state, financial generosity worldwide, long-term governmental benefits, and the comforting Good News of salvation through Jesus Christ from the outstretched hands, open hearts, listening ears, and gentle healing words of the people of God.

Those in need continue to struggle and grieve their many losses. The future sometimes seems hopeless. The obstacles look overwhelming. However, those very needs can point us to our own inability to solve problems by our own strength and wisdom. Confessing our sins and admitting our weakness, we look outside ourselves to the One who created us and sent His only Son to the cross in payment of our sins. He longs to join us with the family of believers through Baptism, where we find hope for the needy, now and eternally.

HURRICANE KATRINA: RESPONSE AS WITNESS

Truly, I say to you, as you did it to one of the least of

these My brothers, you did it to Me. (Matthew 25:40)

The harsh reality of a natural disaster such as Hurricane Katrina, a reality that reveals both the best and the worst of humanity and leaves many people in need, also provides opportunity for Christian response as a witness to the Savior. That response flows from our faith in Jesus alongside other believers and joins the efforts of all others in the nation who are helping to rescue, relieve, and rebuild the affected area of the country. Our response may come in the form of financial contributions, provision of clothing and supplies, becoming a volunteer on location, or opening our homes and churches to displaced persons. Often, when we respond to such crises, we are unaware of how God is using us or why we serve.

In Jesus' famous description of the final judgment, He pictures the separation of the sheep from the goats. Those on the right, the believers in Him by God's grace through faith, He invites to inherit the kingdom prepared for them and commends them for their responses when He was hungry, thirsty, a stranger, naked, sick, and in prison. Totally surprised, these believers ask, "When?" He answers, "Truly, I say to you, as you did it to one of the least of these My brothers, you did it to Me."

In a similar fashion, we simply respond to those in need because of our faith relationship with Christ as Savior. We see Christ in their need, and they see Christ in our response. We have an opportunity to tell them about our Savior and the free gift of eternal life through faith in Him. We give of ourselves with no strings attached. The rest is up to God's Spirit. Response as witness!

God's heart beats in our hearts each day as we praise Him for clothing and shoes, meat and drink, house and home, wife and children, fields, cattle, and all our goods. We pray, "Give us this day our daily bread." We care for the environment, reach out a helping hand, and respond to major world disasters. In many consistent and humble ways as a response to God's love in Christ, we live God's passion for creation. Heartbeat!

CHAPTER 37:

Living God's Passion against Injustice and Idolatry

> Hear me, you heavens! Listen, earth! For
> the LORD has spoken: "I reared children and
> brought them up, but they have rebelled
> against Me." . . . Woe to the sinful nation,
> a people whose guilt is great, a brood of
> evildoers, children given to corruption! They
> have forsaken the LORD; they have spurned the
> Holy One of Israel and turned their backs on
> Him. (Isaiah 1:2, 4 NIV)

In this passage from Isaiah, our Creator, the Holy One of Israel, grieves the rebellion of His creation and of His chosen people, through whom He plans to bring a Messiah to save the world. Therefore, He burns with passion against all sin, especially injustice and idolatry. Throughout Scripture, we see God's holy passion against sin. Paul writes, "For the wrath of God is revealed from heaven against all ungodliness and unrighteousness of men, who by their unrighteousness suppress the truth" (Romans 1:18).

The prophet Isaiah gives concrete expression to God's wrath or passion against human rebellion. What vivid words to describe human sin: "a people loaded with guilt," "a brood of evildoers," "children given to corruption," "spurned the Holy One of Israel," "turned their backs on Him"! The Holy God cannot tolerate such unholiness. Isaiah addresses God's passion against injustice and idolatry in many places. First, one example of injustice, and then one of idolatry. Experience God's passion as you read.

> Woe to those who make unjust laws, to those who issue oppressive decrees, to deprive the poor of their rights and withhold justice from the oppressed of My people, making widows their prey and robbing the fatherless. What will you do on the day of reckoning, when disaster comes from afar? To whom will you run for help? Where will you leave your riches? Nothing will remain but to cringe among the captives or fall among the slain. Yet for all this, His anger is not turned away, His hand is still upraised. (Isaiah 10:1–4 NIV)

> But you—come here, you children of a sorceress, you offspring of adulterers and prostitutes! Who are you mocking? At whom do you sneer and stick out your tongue? Are you not a brood of rebels, the offspring of liars? You burn with lust among the oaks and under every spreading tree; you sacrifice your children in the ravines and under the overhanging crags. The idols among the smooth stones of the ravines are your portion; indeed, they are your lot. Yes, to them you have poured out drink offerings and offered grain offerings. In view of all this, should I relent? (Isaiah 57:3–6 NIV)

Electric words in each example; pointed words that leave no room for interpretation! Isaiah lists specific actions against the poor, the widows, and the orphans, and he proclaims God's condemnation of these sins. The callous laws are labeled as "unjust" and "oppressive." The consequences for such injustice are clear: when the day of reckoning comes with its disaster from afar, you will have nowhere to run for help and will either cringe as a captive or die by the sword. Historically, Judah will first be threatened by the savage Assyrians after they destroy Israel, the Northern Kingdom, and then be destroyed and taken captive by the mighty Babylonian army.

The second example describes idolatry in graphic and ugly terms: high places with Canaanite idols, fertility cults of religious prostitution, and child sacrifice. God's wrath exposes them: they "sneer" and "stick out [their tongues]"; they are "offspring of liars," and they "burn with lust."

With the full force of His passion against idolatry, the Holy One of Israel asks, "Should I relent?"

Isaiah makes clear, however, that God's powerful passion against injustice and idolatry is tempered with great patience because He wants His people to repent and believe in His saving plan through the Messiah:

> Well do I know how treacherous you are; you were called a rebel from birth. For My own name's sake I delay My wrath; for the sake of My praise I hold it back from you, so as not to destroy you completely. See, I have refined you, though not as silver; I have tested you in the furnace of affliction. For My own sake, for My own sake, I do this. (Isaiah 48:8–11 NIV)

Living God's passion for the world takes an uncomfortable turn in this chapter. In many ways, our hearts leap at the opportunity to live His passion for creation, salvation through Jesus, or even reaching all nations through the Church. However, living His passion against injustice and idolatry sounds much more ominous and difficult. We see the evil around us in many different forms. We have our hands full dealing with worldly passions that drain and that lead us into bondage. In fact, we regularly need to confess our own injustice and idolatry. How then can we unite our hearts with God's passion against injustice and idolatry? How can we find the courage to address real issues in our society and world, where God's clear voice needs to be heard? First, we look at the example of Elijah, an Old Testament prophet who displayed incredible courage and who also became a self-pitying fugitive. Then, we observe the backbone of Peter and John facing the religious powers of their day.

ELIJAH: BOLD SPOKESMAN OF GOD

You have abandoned the LORD's commands and have followed the Baals. (1 Kings 18:18b NIV)

No backbone. Always compromising. Blending in with the world. These are valid criticisms of modern Christianity. We often refuse to speak for God, to declare His unfailing Word no matter what the cost. We fail to confront abortion on demand, sexual immorality, injustice toward the have-nots, and abuse of the Word of God.

Elijah was not like that. Called by God in a wicked period of Israel's history, he accepted the challenge of being God's spokesman. Ahab and his evil wife, Jezebel, ruled over Israel and set up altars to Baal. Elijah obeyed God and predicted a punishing drought. Then, at the Lord's command, he went to Ahab and dared to tell him the words of 1 Kings 18:18.

In a dramatic confrontation with the prophets of Baal on Mount Carmel, Elijah said to Israel, "How long will you waver between two opinions? If the LORD is God, follow Him; but if Baal is God, follow him" (verse 21 NIV). Then he called on God to light a spiritual fire on water-drenched wood. God, who had called Elijah, stood by him and brought the victory over the frantic prophets of Baal. The people cried out, "The LORD—He is God! The LORD—He is God!" (verse 39 NIV).

Despite our weakness and compromise, God calls us to speak for Him. In the midst of a wicked world, He sent His own dear Son as the Word made flesh. He both spoke and acted on our behalf. His sacrifice on the cross won the Father's full approval. We cry out with Israel, "The LORD—He is God! The LORD—He is God!" (verse 39 NIV).

Forgiven, we speak His Word—His Word of judgment against sin and evil, and His Word of love and mercy for that same world. Elijah's example points us to God's victory and fortifies us as bold spokespeople of God.

ELIJAH: SELF-PITYING FUGITIVE

Elijah was afraid and ran for his life. . . . "I have had enough, LORD," he said. "Take my life; I am no better than my ancestors." (1 Kings 19:3–4 NIV)

We see another side of Elijah. Though he was a bold spokesman of God on Mount Carmel, we find him running for his life. Threatened by Ahab and Jezebel, he reaches Beersheba, sits down under a broom tree, and wants to die. He engages in self-pity and despair. "I have been very zealous for the LORD God Almighty. The Israelites have rejected Your covenant, broken down Your altars, and put Your prophets to death with the sword. I am the only one left, and now they are trying to kill me too" (verse 10 NIV).

Can you relate to Elijah? We, too, have times of victory, when God seems so real and so powerful. Then come the discouraging moments when we feel surrounded by skeptics, cut off from believers, and scorned for our Christian commitment. Like Elijah, we run away and wallow in self-pity. Lonely, afraid, discouraged, and depressed, we desperately need help.

God helped Elijah, but not in the way he expected. Instead of soothing him and reinforcing his self-pity, God takes him to the holy mountain and speaks to him with "a gentle whisper" (verse 12 NIV). God's Word restores Elijah. He receives instructions for his ongoing ministry but is also assured that he is not alone in Israel. There are still seven thousand who have not gone over to Baal, and Elijah will have Elisha, his successor, to work with him. Elijah receives refreshment for ministry.

God also helps us. He doesn't encourage our self-pitying. He speaks also to us with the gentle whisper of His Word. He reminds us that the Savior has already come and endured the loneliness and rejection of death on a cross for us. He assures us that we are not alone but belong to the fellowship of His people gathered around Word and Sacrament. Then He sends us back to serve Him each day.

BACKBONE

Peter and the apostles answered, "We must obey God rather than men." (Acts 5:29)

We lack backbone. We bend, compromise, give ground, sell out, and look the other direction. Society preaches a new morality, abandons long-held standards, and lives permissively. Abortions on demand, pornography, corruption in high places, and ruthless business practices abound in our country. We lack the courage to stand up and be counted. Spineless wonders!

In the first days after Pentecost, the disciples of Jesus faced stiff opposition from the religious establishment. Peter and John were arrested, brought before the Sanhedrin, and told to keep quiet about their faith in Jesus Christ. They could have played it safe and gone underground. They could have compromised their convictions. Instead, by God's grace, these apostles displayed backbone. Arrested again for preaching Christ crucified, they replied, "We must obey God rather than men." They continued boldly proclaiming the Good News of Jesus. Ultimately, their confession of faith cost most of them their lives as martyrs. God used their testimony to build the Church on the solid foundation of the apostles and prophets, with Jesus Christ as the chief cornerstone. No spineless wonders but by the daily gifts of Baptism, we are bold believers in Christ!

We confess our lack of backbone because of our weak, sinful flesh. He points us to His courageous Son, who endured the cross, despising the shame. With backbone He drove the money-changers out of the temple and exposed the sham of the Pharisees. Risen, He offers us forgiveness and strength to stand up for Him and obey God rather than men. Reinforced by regular use of Word and Sacraments, we step forward with backbone to proclaim Jesus as Savior and Lord in today's society. No longer spineless wonders!

The Word of Christ contains both God's judgment and His mercy. They converge at the cross of Christ. He took upon Himself God's judgment and wrath against sin. As the sinless and obedient Son of God, Jesus' once-for-all sacrifice satisfied God's wrath against sin and expressed the fullness of God's mercy and grace for His creation, now restored. Only through Christ do we find forgiveness and new life. As part of His Church, we proclaim both judgment and mercy—God's Law and Gospel. God wants us to live His passion against injustice and idolatry in today's world so that justice will be done and so that many will be led to confess their injustice and idolatry and receive Christ's forgiveness. God raised up Elijah, Peter, and John to speak His Word with courage. He raises up you and me to speak boldly in our world. Where will you take your stand? With whom will you stand? Stand up for the unborn and those at end of life. Stand against violence at home, in the streets, on the borders, in third world nations. Stand against corruption in governments, businesses, and labor unions. There are many arenas of injustice and idolatry. In every case, because we are sinners, we need to ask whether our passion is prejudiced or reflects God's passion. Only through Christ do we find the source of the strength to act.

"MIDST FLAMING WORLDS"

> I have given them Your word, and the world has hated them because they are not of the world, just as I am not of the world. (John 17:14)

Recently, my wife and I visited the Roman ruins of Pompeii. Through careful reconstruction, the city almost seemed alive, displaying both its luxury and its sinful lifestyle. We were also reminded of its fiery destruction as we viewed plaster casts of a man covering his mouth from the ashes, a pregnant woman hiding, and a dog trying to escape the fiery molten lava of the Mount Vesuvius eruption in AD 79.

The Father's beautiful world, created to serve and praise Him, has been shattered by the ugliness of sin. Satan, the prince of this world, conspires to destroy God's created world by sowing seeds of disobedience and rebellion. John uses that meaning of *world* to describe the human system opposed to God's purposes. We must come to grips with the reality of a sinful world that hates us as it hates Jesus. Those who reject God's love in Jesus face an eternity in the fires of hell.

We are born into a sinful world. By nature we are the children of wrath even as others are. The Holy Spirit, the Counselor, convicts the world of guilt in regard to sin and condemns the prince of this world (John 16:7–11). There is absolutely no room for compromise with the sinful world. As His baptized children through faith in His saving Word, we are set free from this sinful world system, which is led by Satan. We are set free to warn unbelievers of the consequences of their disobedience and to point them to Jesus' blood and righteousness. We are not of the world any more than Jesus is of the world.

For the sake of salvation through Jesus, live God's passion against injustice and idolatry.

Living God's Passion for Salvation through Jesus

> For God so loved the world, that He gave His only Son, that whoever believes in Him should not perish but have eternal life. (John 3:16)

Nowhere does God's passion for the world burn more brightly than in His determination to bring salvation through His only Son, Jesus Christ. Listen to words from the prophet Isaiah about this passion. In the last chapter, we read from the same Book of Isaiah about God's passion against injustice and idolatry. Let God speak from His heart:

> The people who walked in darkness have seen a great light. . . . For to us a child is born, to us a son is given; and the government shall be upon His shoulder, and His name shall be called Wonderful Counselor, Mighty God, Everlasting Father, Prince of Peace. Of the increase of His government and of peace there will be no end, on the throne of David and over His kingdom, to establish it and to uphold it with justice and with righteousness from this time forth and forevermore. The zeal of the LORD of hosts will do this. (Isaiah 9:2, 6–7)

There shall come forth a shoot from the stump of Jesse, and a branch from his roots shall bear fruit. And the Spirit of the LORD shall rest upon Him, the Spirit of wisdom and understanding, the Spirit of counsel and might, the Spirit of knowledge and the fear of the LORD. And His delight shall be in the fear of the LORD. (Isaiah 11:1–3)

On this mountain the LORD of hosts will make for all peoples a feast of rich food, a feast of well-aged wine. . . . He will swallow up death forever; and the Lord GOD will wipe away tears from all faces, and the reproach of His people He will take away from all the earth, for the Lord has spoken. (Isaiah 25:6, 8)

Comfort, comfort My people, says your God. Speak tenderly to Jerusalem, and cry to her that her warfare is ended, that her iniquity is pardoned, that she has received from the LORD's hand double for all her sins. . . . And the glory of the LORD shall be revealed, and all flesh shall see it together, for the mouth of the LORD has spoken. (Isaiah 40:1–2, 5)

Behold My servant, whom I uphold, My chosen, in whom My soul delights; I have put My Spirit upon Him; He will bring forth justice to the nations. (Isaiah 42:1)

The Lord GOD has given Me the tongue of those who are taught, that I may know how to sustain with a word him who is weary. Morning by morning He awakens; He awakens My ear to hear as those who are taught. The Lord GOD has opened My ear, and I was not rebellious; I turned not backward. I gave My back to those who strike, and My cheeks to those who pull out the beard; I hid not My face from disgrace and spitting. But the Lord God helps Me; therefore I have not been disgraced; therefore I have set My face like a flint, and I know that I shall not be put to shame. He who vindicates Me is near. (Isaiah 50:4–8a)

Breathtaking passion from our Creator God who brought us salvation through His only Son, Jesus! Now He calls us to live His passion by sharing that salvation with others.

A SON FOR THE WORLD

I in them and You in Me, that they may become perfectly one, so that the world may know that You sent Me and loved them even as You loved Me. (John 17:23)

The Father's beautiful world was created to serve and praise the one true God: Father, Son, and Holy Spirit. "Flaming worlds" (*LSB* 563:1) are the result of Satan's rebellion, the fall into sin, and a human world system at enmity with God and His creation. Is there any hope for us in this twenty-first century, where we see the effects of the devil, the world, and our sinful flesh upon the nations of the world?

John's simple but powerful words resound through the centuries to bring hope and purpose for life: "For God so loved the world, that He gave His only Son, that whoever believes in Him should not perish but have eternal life" (John 3:16). Jesus adds in His famous High Priestly Prayer, "I in them and You in Me, that they may become perfectly one, so that the world may know that You sent Me and loved them even as You loved Me" (John 17:23).

Jesus came to live a perfect life in our stead and to die on the cross to pay the full punishment for the sins of the whole world.

John applies the word *world* to all people on earth, including those who are opposed to God and "did not know Him" (John 1:10). He forms us believers into His Church, uniting us in the Body of Christ so that the world will know and believe in Jesus as the one sent by the Father to bring salvation.

What a privilege to help the world know Jesus as Savior! We live God's passion for salvation just because the stakes are so high—life or death, salvation or damnation, light or darkness. We unite in love to lift up God's Son for the world!

Consider simple and specific ways you might consider sharing Jesus the Savior as you engage in faith conversations—a favorite Bible verse, the Apostles' Creed, or a well-known hymn verse. Recently, on a cruise, we listened to classical music every evening after dinner, led by the Adagio Strings, a group of four young people whom we got to know. They encouraged requests from a list that they passed around. One evening in that lounge, with clouds and rain outside the window, I requested J. S. Bach's "Jesu, Joy of Man's Desiring." As they played that very evangelical piece, the sun burst through the clouds and remained throughout the performance. A very good conversation starter! On another occasion, I requested "Sheep May Safely Graze" and told the young musicians afterward that this piece by Bach had been played at our wedding almost forty-seven years ago. Another source of witness material for salvation through Jesus might be daily news and magazines in print or electronic format.

BLOOD-RED VISION OF LIFE

For the life of every creature is its blood: its blood is its life. (Leviticus 17:14)

We find words, pictures, and examples in the daily newspaper that help us bear powerful testimony to salvation through Jesus

Christ. During our Saturday morning reflections at the breakfast table, Gail called my attention to *Life: America's Weekend Magazine,* enclosed with that Saturday's newspaper. The bright reds of the cover jumped out at me.

In the foreground of that cover is pictured the visionary digital photographer, Alexander Tsiaras, with his penetrating dark eyes. Surrounding him, you see red and white blood cells magnified 31,000 times, as they swirl through an artery in one of his revolutionary images. The bold question in yellow block print: "Could This Man's Pictures Save Your Life?" Tsiaras has embarked on a mission to depict the human body in all its glory and frailty so you will be inspired to get well—and stay well. Not necessarily based on a Christian vision or even a vision of God's creation, this article with its blood-red pictures provides talking points for our Christian witness.

In Leviticus, the Lord explains to Moses, "For the life of every creature is its blood: its blood is its life." The life-giving nature of blood bears powerful witness to God's marvelous creation, and it lies at the heart of the Old Testament sacrificial system. Most important, this passage points to our redemption through the blood of Christ: "He entered once for all into the holy places, not by means of the blood of goats and calves but by means of His own blood, thus securing an eternal redemption" (Hebrews 9:12).

The *Life* cover and article could help you open up a conversation about a loving God who created life-giving blood for our bodies and forgiveness for our sin through the blood of Christ, a lamb without blemish or spot. To paraphrase, "This man can save your life!" That's a blood-red vision for life.

That vivid magazine article and picture brings us back to the title for this book—*Heartbeat!* God's heart beats from eternity with passion for salvation through Jesus to bring about a new creation for the world through His Church. We don't need to be anxious about sharing Jesus as Savior with others because it does not depend on us, but on Him. He is our life-giver. His heart beats in rhythm with ours. The psalmist puts it this way:

> I bless the LORD who gives me counsel; in the night also my heart instructs me. . . . Therefore my heart is glad, and my whole being rejoices; my flesh also dwells secure. (Psalm 16:7, 9)

Many times we can learn from children about sharing Jesus with others. They simply blurt out a simple story they have learned at home or in church. They may sing a song they have learned. Or they tell the Christmas story by fingering the objects in a nativity scene. One of my grandsons once came up with the idea of creating a Lenten cross out of wood, with holes for purple candles to be lit as the Lenten season unfolds. He probably got the idea from the more common Advent wreath, which also provides witness opportunities.

In fact, when the great theologian Karl Barth was once asked how he would summarize all of Christian theology, his answer was stunning simple: "Jesus loves me! This I know, For the Bible tells me so" ("Jesus Loves Me," *LSB* 588:1). That answer also brings the simple message of *Heartbeat!: Living with Passion in the Word of Christ.*

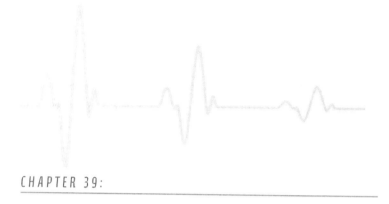

Living God's Passion for Reaching All Nations through the Church

It is too small a thing for You to be My servant
to restore the tribes of Jacob and bring back
those of Israel I have kept. I will also make You
a light for the Gentiles, that My salvation may
reach to the ends of the earth. (Isaiah 49:6 NIV)

God created all nations. All nations rebelled against Him. God sent His Son, Jesus, to die on the cross for all nations. His ongoing passion is for all nations to be saved through faith in Jesus Christ. He has chosen a special people, Old Testament Israel and the New Testament Church, to believe in Him, worship Him, and reach out to all nations with the promised Messiah, who paid the price for the world's sin on Calvary. To Abraham, God promised, "I will bless you and make your name great, so that you will be a blessing. . . . And in you all the families of the earth shall be blessed" (Genesis 12:2–3).

God sends His Suffering Servant, the Messiah, not only to Israel but also through them as a light for the Gentiles so that salvation reaches "to the end of the earth" (Isaiah 49:6).

The risen Christ says to His disciples, "As the Father has sent Me, even so I am sending you" (John 20:21). On the mountain in Galilee, Jesus commands, "Go therefore and make disciples of all nations, baptizing them in the name of the Father and of the Son and of the Holy Spirit, teaching them to observe all that I have commanded you" (Matthew 28:19–20). Right before His ascension into heaven, Jesus adds, "But you will receive power when the Holy Spirit has come upon you, and you will be My witnesses in Jerusalem and in all Judea and Samaria, and to the ends of the earth" (Acts 1:8). Paul and Barnabas quote the Isaiah 49:6 verse when they visit Antioch of Pisidia and find many Gentiles as well as Jews responding to the message of Christ (Acts 13:47). We are told, "And when the Gentiles heard this, they began rejoicing and glorifying the word of the Lord, and as many as were appointed to eternal life believed. And the word of the Lord was spreading throughout the whole region" (Acts 13:48–49).

Can you not feel God's missionary passion for the Church to bring Christ to the world? That passion reverberates throughout Scripture and in the lives of believers today. In what ways has someone lived God's missionary passion for you? A parent, a pastor, a friend, a visiting missionary, a co-worker?

Recently, on a Panama Canal cruise, Gail and I met Robert and Linda, a couple from North Carolina. He has a background in Christian radio after a business career, and she is a concert pianist who lives her faith. We met them at an open-seating table with six others. During that meal, Robert and Linda led the way in Christian conversation as we told our stories of faith in Jesus. They arranged for us to join them for dinner with another couple two days later in order to share more faith conversation. They also place Indonesian pamphlets with a Christian message on tables where Indonesian couples sit as another form of outreach. We have kept in touch with Robert and Linda and have been praying for her grandnephew who has major health problems. They share a missionary passion that has moved us deeply!

Ask yourself some simple questions about your personal mission in life: Whom do you see who is in need of the Good News about salvation through Jesus? What do you hear from people in your life, revealing opportunities for personal caring and witness? How well do you really listen to them? What words come out of your mouth? How well do you speak the timely and encouraging word? How do your actions or inactions bear witness to Jesus in your life? What are you learning about your unique personal mission as you put your faith in action? The searchlight of God's Word exposes our sins and brings us again to Jesus, the light of the world who offers us daily forgiveness and illumines our purpose and path to bring others to faith in Christ in a practical, consistent, and compassionate way.

In our day, we live in the midst of many cultures with people from Africa, Eastern Europe, and the Middle East at our doorstep, university, shopping mall, or place of work. Many are recent immigrants to our land. In what ways might God be opening doors for us to witness of the Savior to them? They need our friendship, caring, and practical help with English and how to adapt to our society. They also have powerful stories to share with us and a wealth of experience. Some organizations in our community, such as Christian Friends of New Americans, help match up needs of new Americans with resources from other Christians.

"ENLARGE MY HEART"

I will run in the way of Your commandments when You enlarge my heart! (Psalm 119:32)

How many times have you heard someone who lives with courage, vision, and generosity described with these words: "He has a big heart!" God's Word enlarges our vision for the Church and the world. Where does it start? Within your heart!

The psalmist puts it simply: "I will run in the way of Your commandments when You enlarge my heart." "In biblical language the heart is the center of the human spirit, from which spring emotions, thought, motivation, courage, and action" *(Concordia Self-Study Bible,* p. 790). Proverbs 4:20–22 counsels that when we are attentive to God's words and keep them within our heart, we receive life and healing. It continues, "Keep your heart with all vigilance, for from it flow the springs of life" (Proverbs 4:23). We will never run to witness until God enlarges our heart. By nature, our hearts are empty and desperately wicked (Jeremiah 17:9). Out of the heart proceed all sorts of evil thoughts—murder, adultery, false witness, and blasphemy (Matthew 15:19). With a repentant David, we cry out, "Create in me a clean heart, O God, and renew a right spirit within me" (Psalm 51:10).

Where does it really start? Within God's heart! From the very heart of God comes His desire for "all people to be saved and to come to the knowledge of the truth" (1 Timothy 2:4). Therefore, He sent His own Son, Jesus, with a pure heart to pay for the world's sin by dying on the cross. In our Baptism, Christ dwells in our hearts through faith (Ephesians 3:17). Through Christ, our hearts are set free, or literally enlarged, because they "swell with joy" (Isaiah 60:5 NIV). Forgiven, restored, and filled with the joy of our salvation, we "run in the way of [God's] commandments" to reach all nations with Christ. Led by the Holy Spirit, our simple prayer today: "Lord, enlarge my heart!"

Indeed, the *Heartbeat!* adventure leads us to live God's passion for the world in His creation, against injustice and idolatry, for salvation through Jesus, and as part of His Church to all nations.

Your *HEARTBEAT!* Adventure

"Christ in you, the hope of glory"
(Colossians 1:27). What a journey of the heart!

You want to live with passion for Christ in all areas of your life, today and over a lifetime. The stories of people living with that passion inspire you to journey on. You begin to see the need to thirst for the Word of Christ each day. God's Word leads you to understand yourself as saint and sinner, unleashing conflicting passions within yourself. God's Spirit has led you to faith in Christ through your Baptism. He gives you that desire to live for Him in witness and service each day, but Satan tempts you to pursue passions that drain and passions that lead to bondage.

Honestly taking stock of these ungodly passions, you have confessed them before God, just as David did, and you have asked for His forgiveness through Christ. Daily forgiven with a clean heart and a right spirit, you have learned how to discover the Word of Christ in fresh ways as you live counter culture and renounce self-help. Hearing God's call, you find your passion in Christ's Passion and rejoice in His Word alive in your daily interactions.

Beyond human belief, you journey deeper in the Word of Christ by craving spiritual milk and eating a steady diet of solid food. In the process, you embrace Christ-help so that you can grow through testing. You have new eyes to see the Word-transformed lives around you, and you begin to build a biblical worldview. As a planting of the Lord for the display of His splendor, you increasingly live God's passion for the world (though you can never fully grasp it). Daily opportunities present themselves for you to live joyfully and productively in God's creation, to stand boldly against injustice and idolatry, to witness one-on-one to salvation through Jesus, and to participate with God's people in a missionary outreach to the nations, abroad and at your doorstep. What one step will you take today? What new venture will you begin for the long term?

Your passion for Christ is simply God's heartbeat for the world! He loves you and the world from eternity, He created a perfect world, He sent His only Son to pay the full price for the world's sin, and He formed a new people of God, the Church, to reach the world with Christ. Your heart beats with God's passion every day and for a lifetime. God bless your *Heartbeat!* adventure, starting today for eternity.

> Let the word of Christ dwell in you richly, teaching and admonishing one another in all wisdom, singing psalms and hymns and spiritual songs, with thankfulness in your hearts to God. And whatever you do, in word or deed, do everything in the name of the Lord Jesus, giving thanks to God the Father through Him. (Colossians 3:16–17)

BIBLIOGRAPHY

Buford, Bob. *Halftime: Moving from Success to Significance.* Grand Rapids: Zondervan Publishing House, 1994. Copyright Robert P. Buford, 1994.

Dömer, Cornelia. *Traveling with Martin Luther: A Tour Guide to the Reformation in Germany,* English translation. St. Louis: Concordia Publishing House, 2010.

Hoffmann, Oswald C. J. *What More Is There to Say but Amen: The Autobiography of Dr. Oswald C. J. Hoffmann as Told to Ronald J. Schlegel.* St. Louis: Concordia Publishing House, 1996.

Mulholland, M. Robert Jr. *Shaped by the Word: The Power of Scripture in Spiritual Formation,* revised edition. Nashville: The Upper Room, 2001. (I am especially indebted to him for his concepts of "How to Read without Reading" and "Breaking the Crust.")

Oesch, Jackie. *Making the Bible Yours: A Journey into the Heart of God.* Longwood, Florida: Xulon Press, 2009. Copyright Full Value Ministries, 2009.

Heartbeat! contains devotional material from two of Dr. Carter's books:

Carter, Stephen J. *My Daily Devotion: God's Promises for Joyful*

Living. St. Louis: Concordia Publishing House, 1988.

Carter, Stephen J. *Witness to the Light: Inspiring Daily Devotions.* St. Louis: Concordia Publishing House, 2006.